THE NEXT VOICE YOU HEAR...

Ladies and gentlemen, I have just been handed a message that came in from Grovers Mill by telephone. Just a moment. At least forty people, including six state troopers, lie dead in a field east of the village of Grovers Mill, their bodies burned and distorted beyond all possible recognition. The next voice you hear will be that of Brigadier General Montgomery Smith, commander of the state militia at Trenton, New Jersey.

General Smith: I have been requested by the governor of New Jersey to place the counties of Mercer and Middlesex as far west as Princeton, and east to Jamesburg, under martial law. No one will be permitted to enter this area except by special pass issued by state or military authorities. Four companies of state militia are proceeding from Trenton to Grovers Mill, and will aid in the evacuation . . .

They cut every telegraph and wrecked the railways.

HOWARD KOCH
THE PANIC BROADCAST

 AVON
PUBLISHERS OF BARD, CAMELOT, DISCUS, EQUINOX AND

The play *"Invasion From Mars"* included in this book
was copyrighted in 1940 by Hadley Cantril,
© renewed 1967 by Howard Koch.

The hardcover edition of this book was published by
agreement with Manheim Fox Enterprises, Inc.

AVON BOOKS
A division of
The Hearst Corporation
959 Eighth Avenue
New York, New York 10019

Copyright © 1970 by Howard Koch.
Published by arrangement with Little, Brown and Company.
Library of Congress Catalog Card Number: 73-121433.

Sixth Avon Printing

ISBN: 0–380-00501-8

AVON TRADEMARK REG. U.S. PAT. OFF. AND
FOREIGN COUNTRIES, REGISTERED TRADEMARK—
MARCA REGISTRADA, HECHO EN CHICAGO, U.S.A.

Printed in the U.S.A.

To Hardy and Karyl

PICTURE CREDITS

THE
PANIC
BROADCAST

INTRODUCTION

In 1898 H. G. Wells published a novella entitled *The War of the Worlds* about an invasion of the earth by creatures from the planet Mars which I dramatized in the form of news bulletins and the diary of a survivor. On the Eve of Hallowe'en, October 30, 1938, this radio play was broadcast over CBS by Orson Welles and the Mercury Theatre with some startling and unforeseen results. Over the intervening years the event has been commemorated on its anniversary in various radio and television programs as part of American folklore. Since Mars is much in the news today, it seemed an appropriate time to chronicle some of the happenings before, during and after the broadcast as recalled by one of its many contributors.

Unless we give credence to the so-called flying saucers, no beings from outer space have yet appeared on earth; the traffic appears to be the other way. Having already landed on the moon, man is reaching out toward Mars and the other planets.

One of the foremost authorities on space exploration is Arthur C. Clarke, former chairman of the British Interplanetary Society and Fellow of the Royal Astronomical Society. Some of his early works on the problems of space travel have become university textbooks on the subject but perhaps he is best known in this country as the author of science fiction, including a story which provided the material for the Stanley Kubrick film, 2001.

I first met Arthur Clarke in London in 1953 when he supplied technical information on space flight which I needed for a science fiction film. At the time he predicted that men would orbit the earth within ten years and land on the moon within twenty. So in addition to his many other accomplishments, he is something of a prophet.

Since he also wrote a story about outer-space visitors to the earth, although their mission was quite different from the Martians in the broadcast, I felt his thoughts on the subject would be enlightening. The following interview, which took place on October 19, 1969, records some of his views.

Howard Koch: Some seventeen years ago you wrote *Childhood's End* which many consider the classic of science fiction. In your story the Overlords or Guardians, arriving on earth from some planet in outer space, were benevolent beings whose purpose was to prevent the human race from destroying itself. In the H. G. Wells story the Martians were violent and destructive in-

Wells . . . . Welles

"How odd"   "Amazing"

vaders. If beings actually do arrive from other worlds, do you believe they would be apt to be monstrous as Wells portrayed them or highly civilized and sympathetic as you imagined them in your novel?

Arthur Clarke: I think that the sort of unmotivated malevolence which is typical of many science fiction stories is unlikely because some of the invaders in space that we've encountered in fiction would simply have destroyed themselves before they got anywhere else. And as I've suggested in quite a few essays, with a very high intelligence would also go higher moral values because, without these, intelligence is self-destructive. However, at the same time, one must admit that in a practically infinite universe almost anything is theoretically possible to happen somewhere. One can imagine, for example, a case where even a benevolent and intelligent race, if it lost its home planet, would have no alternative, or at least think it had no alternative, but to conquer another solar system. I think this is unlikely but certainly not impossible.

H.K.: Mars seems to be regarded as the next target in space after the moon. Do you think we should expend the money and effort to attempt a manned landing on the planet during the next decade?

A.C.: Oh, certainly not during the next decade. That would be quite premature. First we have to develop the space station for many down-to-earth applications and, as we develop space stations and work out techniques for long sustenance in space and light support systems for periods of several years, then we'll automatically generate the technology needed to go to Mars. And the time will be right, probably at the end of this decade, to plan a mission and sometime in the eighties it should be quite feasible.

H.K.: Do you believe there's any likelihood of some form of organic life on Mars?

A.C.: A very considerable likelihood. Nothing we've discovered about Mars has ruled that out. On the other hand, we've known for some time there's no possibility of higher animal life forms similar to those on earth. There may be higher life forms but they'll be quite different from anything we have here. And the vegetation and microorganisms could flourish on Mars without any problem, assuming they ever had a chance of getting started there.

H.K.: If such an expedition is launched to reach Mars, what benefits to mankind can we expect?

A.C.: Well, we just don't know yet. The benefits, as far as we can see, will be largely scientific and they will be enormous because any discovery on a new planet produces vast quantities of knowledge which is valuable as part of man's heritage and which inevitably has all sorts of unexpected repercussions and practical applications which can never be foreseen in advance. I feel reasonably sure we'll be living on Mars some day and many

7

people will eventually call it home and perhaps look down on earth as a terrible place and be glad they're on Mars.

H.K.: As Arthur Clarke has projected us into the future, we will now go back in time to an October night in the year 1938 . . .

THE NIGHT THE WORLD
CAME TO AN END — ALMOST

In a sense I myself was one of the victims . . .

The 30th of October before the outbreak of World War II will be remembered as that extraordinary night when the submerged anxieties of tens of thousands of Americans surfaced and coalesced in a flood of terror that swept the country. Between nine o'clock eastern standard time and dawn of the next day men, women and children in scores of towns and cities across the nation were in flight from objects that had no existence except in their imaginations.

I was an astonished contributor to this bizarre event which still occupies students of social psychology searching for clues why rational behavior was suspended on such a vast scale. In the course of forty-five minutes of actual time — as differentiated from subjective or fictional time — the invading Martians were presumably able to blast off from their planet, land on the earth, set up their destructive machines, defeat our army, disrupt communications, demoralize the population and occupy whole sections of the country. In forty-five minutes!

At the time I was a young playwright doing my first professional job, which was writing the radio plays for the Mercury Theatre's Sunday evening programs sponsored by CBS and which were built around the name and talents of Orson Welles. It was an experience lasting six months I wouldn't have missed nor would want to go through again.

Each week by rehearsal time I was responsible for sixty pages of script dramatizing some literary work — usually a novel or short story — assigned to me by Orson or his co-producer, John Houseman, both of whom had pretty exacting standards. They considered sleep a luxury which, for the most part, they denied themselves as well as their staff. Early morning until late at night my pencil sped and, as energies dwindled, crawled over the yellow pages of my pad to be transcribed by the young college-girl-of-all-work who somehow learned to read my scrawl. Each batch of fifteen or twenty pages would be rushed over to Welles and Houseman for their criticisms and suggestions. Then came the revisions, and the revisions of the revisions ad infinitum until the deadline Sunday noon when Orson took over at rehearsals and worked his particular magic. The Girl Friday and I used to ponder how our two bosses were apparently thriving on this strenuous regime, gaining weight while the pounds were oozing off us. And for my part in all this I received the lordly sum of seventy-five dollars a week. (Only later did I realize that the fringe benefits of training and discipline were worth many times my salary.)

A day came when a novella was handed me — H. G. Wells's *The War of the Worlds* — with instructions from Houseman to dramatize it in the form of news bulletins. Reading the story, which was laid in England and written in narrative style, I realized I could use practically nothing but the author's idea of a Martian invasion and his description of their appearance and their machines. In short, I was being asked to do an almost entirely original hour-length play in six days. I called Houseman, pleading to have the assignment changed to another subject. He talked to Orson and called back. The answer was a firm no, this was Orson's favorite project.

On Monday, my one day off, I made a quick trip up the Hudson to see my family. On the way back it occurred to me I needed a map to establish the location of the first Martian arrivals. I drove into a gas station and, since I was on Route 9 W where it goes through a part of New Jersey, the attendant gave me a map of that state.

Back in New York starting to work, I spread out the map, closed my eyes and put down the pencil point. It happened to fall on Grovers Mill. I liked the sound, it had an authentic ring. Also it was near Princeton where I could logically bring in the observatory and the astronomer, Professor Pierson, who became a leading character in the drama.

13

Little did I suspect when I made that haphazard choice that in the days following the broadcast an enterprising farmer in Grovers Mill would be charging a fifty cent parking fee for the hundreds of cars that swarmed on his farm bringing tourists who wanted to see the spot "where the Martians landed." Early this year — three decades later — a news item in the *Times* reported a real estate development in Grovers Mill where building lots were being offered at fancy prices because their location was advertised as the historical site of the Martian invasion.

The six days before the broadcast were one nightmare of scenes written and rewritten between frantic telephone calls and pages speeding back and forth to the studio and, all the while, that Sunday deadline staring me in the face. Once the Martians had landed, I deployed the opposing forces over an ever-widening area, made moves and countermoves between the invaders and the defenders; eventually I found myself enjoying the destruction I was wreaking like a drunken general. Finally, after demolishing the Columbia Broadcasting Building, perhaps a subconscious wish fulfillment, I ended the holocaust with one lonely ham radio voice on the air, "Isn't there anyone on the air? Isn't there anyone."

By that time it seems that only the hardiest souls, or those who knew it was a play, were still listening. People were fleeing blindly in every direction on foot and in all kinds of vehicles. The scene in Newark, as it was later described to me, was one of complete chaos, hundreds of cars racing down streets, disregarding traffic lights to the bafflement of policemen like a Keystone Comedy. Since by this time my fictional Martians were landing all over the country, it is difficult to understand the advantage of flight but in a panic situation adrenalin, not reason, becomes the motor power governing behavior. And as thirst can create mirages on the desert, fear can conjure up sensory images that have no objective reality. People in the Riverside area reported to the bewildered police the sighting of Martians on their giant machines poised on the Jersey Palisades before wading the Hudson to take possession of New York City.

In a sense I myself was one of the victims of the "Hallowe'en prank" as Orson later called it in a masterly understatement. After listening to the broadcast in my apartment, I went to sleep, blissfully unaware of what was happening outside. Houseman called later that night to break the news but I was too exhausted to hear the telephone ring. The next morning — blessed Monday, when I could afford the time for a haircut — I walked down Seventy-second Street on my way to the barbershop. There was an air of excitement among the passersby. Catching ominous snatches of conversation with words like "invasion" and "panic," I jumped to the conclusion that Hitler had invaded some new territory and that the war we all dreaded had finally broken out.

D**A**ILY NEWS ★★★★ FINAL

Vol. 20. No. 109   New York, Monday, October 31, 1938*   48 Pages   2 Cents

FAKE RADIO 'WAR' STIRS TERROR THROUGH U.S.

New York World-Telegram

AND THE EVENING MAIL
A SCRIPPS-HOWARD NEWSPAPER.

Y W. HOWARD, President and Editor; LEE B WOOD,
cutive Editor; MERLIN H. AYLESWORTH, Publisher;
S. MACNEISH, Business Manager.

Phone BArclay 7-3211.

Owned and published daily (except Sunday) by New
York World-Telegram Corpora-
tion. Main office, 125 Barclay
Street. Branch office, 141 West
42nd Street, corner Broadway
(Room 204).

SCRIPPS-HOWARD

Member of United Press Associated Press. Scripps - Howard
Newspaper Alliance NEA Service,
Inc.; Newspaper Information
Service, which organizations re-
tain exclusive rights to all news
and features credited to them.
Member of the Audit Bureau of
Circulations. The Associated Press
is exclusively entitled to the use
for republication of all news
dispatches credited to it or not
otherwise credited in this paper

Subscription rate by mail for
New York World-Telegram in the
United States (outside of New
York City), one year, $12.00.

TUESDAY, NOVEMBER 1, 1938.

Frighted with False Fire."

It is strange and disturbing that thousands
Americans, secure in their homes on a
niet Sunday evening, could be scared out of
teir wits by a radio dramatization of H. G.
ells' fantastic old story, "The War of the
orlds."

We're sure the 23-year-old actor, Orson
elles, didn't realize the panic he was
reading from coast to coast among people
no believed that monsters from Mars
tually had invaded New Jersey.

Yet young Mr. Welles, a student of
akespeare, might have remembered Hamlet
d, remembering, might have foreseen the
ect of too much dramatic realism on an
dience already strung to high nervous

Hamlet it was who staged a play to "catch
e conscience" of the King of Denmark, his

uncle, who had murdered Hamlet's father,
seized the throne and married the widowed
queen. This play within a play also concerned
the murder of a king. This play within a play also concerned
tended, his uncle and his mother were driven
to such hysterical terror that they refused to
watch it to the end.

"What, frighted with false fire!" exclaimed
Hamlet with bitter scorn, certain now of his
uncle's guilt.

Unlike Hamlet, young Mr. Welles did not
plan deliberately to demoralize his audience.
And no guilty consciences, but nerves made
jittery by actual, though almost incredible,
threats of war and disaster, had prepared a
good many American radio listeners to believe the completely incredible "news" that
Martian hordes were here.

Of course it should never happen again.
But we don't agree with those who are argu-
ing that the Sunday night scare shows a need
for strict government censorship of radio
programs.

On the contrary, we think it is evidence
of how dangerous political control of radio
might become. If so many people could be
misled unintentionally, when the purpose was
merely to entertain, what could designing
politicians not do through control of broadcasting stations.

The dictators in Europe use radio to make
their people believe falsehoods. We want
nothing like that here. Better have American
radio remain free to make occasional blunders
than start on a course that might, in time, de-
prive it of freedom to broadcast uncensored
truth.

And it should be easy for radio to avoid
repeating this particular blunder. The Columbia system, as a result of its unhappy experience Sunday night, has already pointed the
way. Let all chains, all stations, avoid use of
the news broadcasting technique in dramatiza-
tions when there is any possibility of any
listener mistaking fiction for fact.

VOL. LXXXVIII...No. 29,500.   Entered as Second-Class Matter, Postoffice, New York, N. Y.   NEW YORK, MONDAY, OCTOBER 31, 1938.   P P   THREE CENTS NEW YORK CITY | FOUR CENTS Elsewhere Except and Vicinity | in 7th and 8th Postal Zones

Radio Listeners in Panic, Taking War Drama as Fact

Many Flee Homes to Escape 'Gas Raid From Mars'—Phone Calls Swamp Police at Broadcast of Wells Fantasy

A wave of mass hysteria seized thousands of radio listeners throughout the nation between 8:15 and 9:30 o'clock last night when a broadcast of a dramatization of H. G. Wells's fantasy, "The War of the Worlds," led thousands to believe that an interplanetary conflict had started with invading Martians spreading wide death and destruction in New Jersey and New York.

The broadcast, which disrupted households, interrupted religious services, created traffic jams and clogged communications systems, was made by Orson Welles, who as the radio character, "The Shadow," used to give "the creeps" to countless child listeners. This time at least a score of adults required medical treatment for shock and hysteria.

In Newark, in a single block at Heddon Terrace and Hawthorne Avenue, more than twenty families

which it is a part. The simulated program began. A weather report was given, prosaically. An announcer remarked that the program would be continued from a hotel, with dance music. For a few moments a dance program was given in the usual manner. Then there was a "break-in" with a "flash" about a professor at an observatory noting a series of gas explosions on the planet Mars.

News bulletins and scene broadcasts followed, with the technique in which the radio had reported actual events, the landing of a "meteor" near Princeton, N. J., "killing" 1,500 persons, the discovery that the "meteor" was a "metal cylinder" containing strange creatures from Mars armed with "death rays" to open hostilities against the inhabitants of the earth.

Despite the fantastic nature of the reported "occurrences," the program, coming less than a month after the recent war scare in Europe and a period in which the radio frequently interrupted regularly scheduled programs to report developments in the Czechoslovak situation, caused

From one New York theatre a manager reported that a throng of playgoers had rushed from his theatre as a result of the broadcast. He said that the wives of two men in the audience, having heard the broadcast, called the theatre and insisted that their husbands, be paged. This spread the "news" to others in the audience.

The switchboard of THE NEW YORK TIMES was overwhelmed by the calls. A total of 875 were received. One man who called from Dayton, Ohio, asked, "What time will it be the end of the world?" A caller from the suburbs said he had had a houseful of guests and all had rushed out to the yard for safety.

Warren Dean, a member of the American Legion living in Manhattan, who telephoned to verify the "reports," expressed indignation which was typical of that of many callers.

"I've heard a lot of radio programs, but I've never heard anything as rotten as that," Mr. Dean said. "It was too realistic for comfort. They broke into a dance pro-

shouting that enemy planes were crossing the Hudson River and asking what he should do. A man came in to the West 152d Street Station, seeking traffic directions. The broadcast became a rumor that spread through the district and many persons stood on street corners hoping for a sight of the "battle" in the skies.

In Queens the principal question asked of the switchboard operators at Police Headquarters was whether "the wave of poison gas will reach as far as Queens." Many said they were all packed up and ready to leave Queens when told to do so.

Samuel Tishman of 100 Riverside Drive was one of the multitude that fled into the street after hearing part of the program. He declared that hundreds of persons evacuated their homes fearing that the "city was being bombed."

"I came home at 9:15 P. M. just in time to receive a telephone call from my nephew who was frantic with fear. He told me the city was about to be bombed from the air and advised me to get out of the building at once. I turned on the

...ized motor dashed furniture.

Throughout New York families left their homes, some to flee to near-by parks. Thousands of persons called the police, newspapers and radio stations here and in other cities of the United States and Canada seeking advice on protective measures against the raids.

The program was produced by Mr. Welles and the Mercury Theatre on the Air over station WABC and the Columbia Broadcasting System's coast-to-coast network, from 8 to 9 o'clock.

The radio play, as presented, was to simulate a regular radio program with a "break-in" for material of the play. The radio listeners, apparently, missed or did not listen to the introduction, which was: "The Columbia Broadcasting System and its affiliated stations present Orson Welles and the Mercury Theatre on the Air in 'The War of the Worlds' by H. G. Wells."

They also failed to associate the program with the newspaper listing of the program, announced as "Today: 8:00-9:00—Play: H. G. Wells's War of the Worlds'—WABC." They ignored three additional announcements made during the broadcast emphasizing its fictional nature.

Mr. Welles opened the program with a description of the series of

sought first to verify the reports. But large numbers, obviously in a state of terror, asked how they could follow the broadcast's advice and flee from the city, whether they would be safer in the cellar or on the roof, how they could safeguard their children, and many of the questions which had been worrying residents of London and Paris during the tense days before the Munich agreement.

So many calls came to newspapers and so many newspapers found it advisable to check on the reports despite their fantastic content that The Associated Press sent out the following at 8:48 P. M.:

"Note to Editors: Queries to newspapers from radio listeners throughout the United States tonight, regarding a reported meteor fall which killed a number of New Jerseyites, are the result of a studio dramatization. The A. P."

Similarly police teletype systems carried notices to all stationhouses, and police short-wave radio stations notified police radio cars that the event was imaginary.

Message From the Police

The New York police sent out the following:

"To all receivers: Station WABC informs us that the broadcast just concluded over that station was a dramatization of a play. No cause for alarm."

The New Jersey State Police teletyped the following:

"Note to all receivers—WABC broadcast as drama re this section being attacked by residents of Mars. Imaginary affair."

the West Forty-seventh Street police station dragging two children, all carrying extra clothing. She said she was ready to leave the city. Police persuaded her to stay.

A garbled version of the reports reached the Dixie Bus Terminal, causing officials there to prepare to change their schedule on confirmation of "news" of an accident at Princeton on their New Jersey route. Miss Dorothy Brown at the terminal sought verification, however, when the caller refused to talk with her that "the world is coming to an end and I have a lot to do."

Harlem Shaken By the "News"

Harlem was shaken by the "news." Thirty men and women rushed into the West 123d Street police station and twelve into the West 135th Street station saying they had packed their household goods and were all ready to leave Harlem if the police would tell them where to go to be "evacuated." One man insisted he had heard "the President's voice" over the radio advising all citizens to leave the cities.

The parlor churches in the Negro district, congregations of the smaller sects meeting on the ground floors of brownstone houses, took the "news" in stride as less faithful parishioners rushed in with it, seeking spiritual consolation. Evening services became "end of the world" prayer meetings in some.

One man ran into the Wadsworth Avenue Police Station in Washington Heights, white with terror,

street there were hundreds of people milling around in panic. Most of us ran toward Broadway and taxi drivers who had heard the entire broadcast on their radios that we knew what it was all about. It was the most asinine stunt I ever heard of."

"I heard that broadcast and almost had a heart attack," said Louis Winkler of 1,322 Clay Avenue, the Bronx. "I didn't tune it in until the program was half over, but when I heard the names and titles of Federal, State and municipal officials and when the 'Secretary of the Interior' was introduced, I was convinced that it was the McCoy. I ran out into the street with scores of others, and found people running in all directions. The whole thing came over as a news broadcast and in my mind it was a pretty crummy thing to do."

The Telegraph Bureau switchboard at police headquarters in Manhattan, operated by thirteen men, was so swamped with calls from apprehensive citizens inquiring about the broadcast that police business was seriously interfered with.

Headquarters, unable to reach the radio station by telephone, sent a radio patrol car there to ascertain the reason for the reaction to the program. When the explanation was given, a police message was sent to all precincts in the five boroughs advising the commands of the cause.

Continued on Page Four

RADIO WAR DRAMA CREATES A PANIC

Continued From Page One

"They're Bombing New Jersey!"

Patrolman John Morrison was on duty at the switchboard in the Bronx Police Headquarters when, as he afterward expressed it, all the lines became busy at once. Among the first who answered was a man who informed him:

"They're bombing New Jersey!"

"How do you know?" Patrolman Morrison inquired.

"I heard it on the radio," the voice at the other end of the wire replied. "Then I went to the roof and I could see the smoke from the bombs, drifting over toward New York. What shall I do?"

The patrolman calmed the caller as well as he could, then answered other inquiries from persons who wanted to know whether the reports of a bombardment were true, and if so where they should take refuge.

At Brooklyn police headquarters, eight men assigned to the monitor switchboard estimated that they had answered more than 300 inquiries from persons who had been alarmed by the broadcast. A number of these, the police said, came from motorists who had heard the program over their car radios and

Because some of the inmates took the catastrophic reports seriously as they came over the radio, some of the hospitals and the county penitentiary ordered that the radios be turned off.

Thousands of calls came in to Newark Police Headquarters. These were not only from the terror-stricken. Hundreds of physicians and nurses, believing the reports to be true, called to "volunteer" their services to aid the "injured." City officials also called in to make "emergency" arrangements for the population. Radio cars were stopped by the panicky throughout that city.

Jersey City police headquarters received similar calls. One woman asked Detective Timothy Grooty, on duty there, "Shall I close my windows?" A man asked, "Have the police any extra gas masks?" Many of the callers, on being assured the reports were fiction, queried again and again, uncertain in whom to believe.

Scores of persons in lower Newark Avenue, Jersey City, left their homes and stood fearfully in the street, looking with apprehension toward the sky. A radio car was dispatched there to reassure them.

The incident at Hedden Terrace and Hawthorne Avenue, in Newark, one of the most dramatic in the area, caused a tie-up in traffic for blocks around. There more than twenty families there apparently believed the "gas attack" had started, and so reported to the

with calls for more than an hour and the company did not have time to summon emergency operators to relieve the congestion. Hardest hit was the Trenton toll office, which handled calls from all over the East.

One of the radio reports, the statement about the mobilization of 7,000 national guardsmen in New Jersey, caused the armories in New Jersey, Sussex and Essex counties to be swamped with calls from officers and men seeking information about the mobilization place.

Prayers for Deliverance

In Caldwell, N. J., an excited parishioner ran into the First Baptist Church during evening services and shouted that a meteor had fallen, showering death and destruction, and that North Jersey was threatened. The Rev. Thomas Thomas, the pastor quieted the congregation and all prayed for deliverance from the "catastrophe."

East Orange police headquarters received more than 200 calls from persons who wanted to know what to do to escape the "gas." Unaware of the broadcast, the switchboard operator tried to telephone Newark, but was unable to get the call through because the switchboard at Newark headquarters was tied up. The mystery was not cleared up until a teletype explanation had been received from Trenton.

More than 100 calls were received at Maplewood police headquarters

WASHINGTON, Oct. 30.—Informed of the furore created tonight by the broadcasting of the Wells drama, "War of the Worlds," officials of the Federal Communications Commission indicated that the commission might review the broadcast.

The usual practice of the commission is not to investigate broadcasts unless formal demands for an inquiry are made, but the commission has the power, officials pointed out, to initiate proceedings where the public interest seems to warrant official action.

his community, including children. He said he knew of one woman who ran into the street with her two children and asked for the help of neighbors in saving them.

"We were sitting in the living room casually listening to the radio," he said, "when we heard reports of a meteor falling near New Brunswick and reports that gas was spreading. Then there was an announcement from the Secretary of Interior from Washington who spoke of the happening as a major disaster. It was the worst thing I ever heard over the air."

Columbia Explains Broadcast

seemed to come from women.

The National Broadcasting Company reported that men stationed at the WJZ transmitting station at Bound Brook, N. J., had received dozens of calls from residents of that area. The transmitting station communicated with New York and passed the information that there was no cause for alarm to the persons who inquired later.

Meanwhile the New York telephone operators of the company found their switchboards swamped with incoming demands for information, although the NBC system had no part in the program.

Record Westchester Calls

The State, county, parkway and local police in Westchester County were swamped also with calls from terrified residents. Of the local police departments, Mount Vernon, White Plains, Mount Kisco, Yonkers and Tarrytown received most of the inquiries. At first the authorities thought they were being made the victims of a practical joke, but when the calls persisted and increased in volume they began to make inquiries. The New York Telephone Company reported that it had never handled so many calls in one hour in years in Westchester.

One man called the Mount Vernon Police Headquarters to find out "where the forty policemen were killed"; another said his brother was ill in bed listening to the broadcast and when he heard the reports he got into an automobile and "disappeared." "I'm nearly crazy!" the caller exclaimed.

They found the families with wet cloths on faces contorted with hysteria. The police calmed them, helped those who were attempting to move their furniture out on their cars and after a time were able to clear the traffic snarl.

At St. Michael's Hospital, High Street and Central Avenue, in the heart of the Newark industrial district, fifteen men and women were treated for shock and hysteria. In some cases it was necessary to give sedatives, and nurses and physicians sat down and talked with the more seriously affected.

While this was going on, three persons with children under treatment in the institution telephoned that they were taking them out and leaving the city, but their fears were calmed when hospital authorities explained what had happened.

A flickering of electric lights in Bergen County from about 6:15 to 6:30 last evening provided a build-up for the terror that was to ensue when the radio broadcast started.

Without going out entirely, the lights dimmed and brightened alternately and radio reception was also affected. The Public Service Gas and Electric Company was mystified by the behavior of the lights, declaring there was nothing wrong at their power plants or in their distributing system. A spokesman for the service department said a call was made to Newark and the same situation was reported. He believed, he said, that the condition was general throughout the State.

The New Jersey Bell Telephone Company reported that every central office in the State was flooded

get back to their homes now that the Pulaski Skyway had been blown up.

The women and children were crying and it took some time for the police to convince them that the catastrophe was fictitious. Many persons who called Maplewood said their neighbors were packing their possessions and preparing to leave the country.

In Orange, N. J., an unidentified man rushed into the lobby of the Lido Theatre, a neighborhood motion picture house, with the intention of "warning" the audience that a meteor had fallen on Raymond Boulevard, Newark, and was spreading poisonous gases. Skeptical, Al Hochberg, manager of the theatre, prevented the man from entering the auditorium and then called the police. He was informed that the radio broadcast was responsible for the man's alarm.

Emanuel Priola, bartender of a tavern at 442 Valley Road, West Orange, closed the place, sending away six customers, in the middle of the broadcast to "rescue" his wife and two children.

"At first I thought it was a lot of Buck Rogers stuff, but when a friend telephoned me that general orders had been issued to evacuate every one from the metropolitan area I put the customers out, closed the place and started to drive home," he said.

William H. Decker of 20 Aubrey Road, Montclair, N. J., denounced the broadcast as "a disgrace" and "an outrage," which he said had frightened hundreds of residents in

which was broadcast "followed the original closely, but to make the imaginary details more interesting to American listeners the adapter, Orson Welles, substituted an American locale for the English scenes of the story."

Pointing out that the fictional character of the broadcast had been announced four times and had been previously publicized, it continued:

"Nevertheless, the program apparently was produced with such vividness that some listeners who may have heard only fragments thought the broadcast was fact, not fiction. Hundreds of telephone calls reaching CBS stations, city authorities, newspaper offices and police headquarters in various cities testified to the mistaken belief.

"Naturally, it was neither Columbia's nor the Mercury Theatre's intention to mislead any one, and when it became evident that a part of the audience had been disturbed by the performance five announcements were read over the network later in the evening to reassure those listeners."

Expressing profound regret that his dramatic efforts should cause such consternation, Mr. Welles said: "I don't think we will choose anything like this again." He hesitated about presenting it, he disclosed, because "it was our thought that perhaps people might be bored or annoyed at hearing a tale so improbable."

Fake 'War' On Radio Spreads Panic Over U.S.

By GEORGE DIXON.

A radio dramatization of H. G. Wells' "War of the Worlds"—which thousands of people misunderstood as a news broadcast of a current catastrophe in New Jersey—created almost unbelievable scenes of terror in New York, New Jersey, the South and as far west as San Francisco between 8 and 9 o'clock last night.

The panic started when an announcer s u d d e n l y interrupted the program of a dance orchestra—which was part of the dramatization—to "flash" an imaginary bulletin that a mysterious "meteor" had struck New Jersey, lighting the heavens for miles around.

A few seconds later, the announcer "flashed" the tidings that weird monsters were swarming out of the mass of metal—which was not a meteor but a tube-like car from Mars — and were destroying hundreds of people with death-ray guns.

Thousands Flee.

Without waiting for further details, thousands of listeners rushed from their homes in New York and New Jersey, many with towels across their faces to protect themselves from the "gas" which the invader was supposed to be spewing forth.

Simultaneously, thousands more in states that stretched west to California and south to the Gulf of Mexico rushed to their telephones to inquire of newspapers, the police, switchboard operators, and electric companies what they should do to protect themselves.

The "space cartridge" was supposed to have struck at Grover's Mills, an actual town near Princeton. Names of well-known highways were used in describing the advance of the monsters. The "Governor of New Jersey" declared martial law and the "Secretary of the Interior" tried to calm the people.

1,100 Call News.

Eleven hundred calls flooded the switchboard at The News—more than when the dirigible Hindenburg exploded.

Occupants of Park Ave. apartment houses flocked to the street.

In Harlem excited cro shouted that President Roosev

(Continued on page 6, col. 1)

Senator Maps Bill t Censor Air Wave

Des Moines, Oct. 30 (AP).—Se ator Clyde L. Herring (Dem Iowa) said tonight he plann to introduce a bill in the ne session of Congress "controlli just such abuses as was hea over the radio tonight." He sa the bill would propose a censo ship board to which all rad programs must be submitted.

Frank R. McNinch, chairm of the Federal Communicatio Commission, in Washington, sa that an investigation would held at once by the FCC. would not predict what acti might be taken, but said a tho ough probe would be made.

War's Over
How U. S. Met Mars

The radio's "end of the world," as some listeners understood it, produced repercussions throughout the United States. Samples, as reported by the Associated Press, follow:

Woman Tries Suicide

Pittsburgh.—A man returned home in the midst of the broadcast and found his wife, a bottle of poison in her hand, screaming: "I'd rather die this way than like that."

Man Wants to Fight Mars

San Francisco.—An offer to volunteer in stopping an invasion from Mars came among hundreds of telephone inquiries to police and newspapers during the radio dramatization of H. G. Wells' story. One excited man called Oakland police and shouted: "My God! Where can I volunteer my services? We've got to stop this awful thing!"

Church Lets Out

Indianapolis.—A woman ran into a church screaming: "New York destroyed; it's the end of the world. You might as well go home to die. I just heard it on the radio." Services were dismissed immediately.

College Boys Faint

Brevard, N. C.—Five Brevard College students fainted and panic gripped the campus for a half hour with many students fighting for telephones to inform their parents to come and get them.

It's a Massacre

Providence, R. I.—Weeping and hysterical women swamped the switchboard of the Providence Journal for details of the "massacre." The electric company received scores of calls urging it to turn off all lights so that the city would be safe from the "enemy."

She Sees "the Fire"

Boston.—One woman declared she could "see the fire" and told the Boston Globe she and many others in her neighborhood were "getting out of here."

"Where Is It Safe?"

Kansas City.—One telephone informant said he had loaded all his children into his car, had filled it with gasoline, and was going somewhere. "Where is it safe?" he wanted to know. The Associated Press bureau received queries on the "meteors" from Los Angeles, Salt Lake City, Beaumont, Tex., and St. Joseph, Mo.

Prayers in Richmond

Richmond, Va.—The Times-Dispatch reported some of its telephone calls came from persons who said they were praying.

Atlanta's "Monsters"

Atlanta—Listeners throughout the Southeast called newspapers reporting that "a planet struck in New Jersey, with monsters and almost everything, and anywhere from 40 to 7,000 people were killed." Editors said responsible persons, known to them, were among the anxious information seekers.

Rushes Home From Reno

Reno.—Marion Leslie Thorgaard, here for a divorce from Hilsee Robert Thorgaard, of New York, collapsed, fearing her mother and children in New York had been killed. One man, immediately started East in hope of aiding the wife he was here to divorce.

When I anxiously questioned the barber, he broke into a broad grin, "Haven't you heard?" and he held up the front page of a morning newspaper with the headline "Nation in Panic from Martian Broadcast." This was a moment that still seems unreal to me. I stared at the paper while the confused barber stared at me. Center page was a picture of Orson, his arms outstretched in a gesture of helpless innocence, and underneath was the opening scene of my play.

For twenty-four hours after the broadcast the fates of all of us who had participated hung in the balance. The public couldn't make up its collective mind whether we were heroes or villains. While there were numerous injuries, miraculously no one actually died in the mad scramble to escape the Martians although one woman was reported in the act of taking poison but stopped in time by her husband. Then Dorothy Thompson in her influential column gave the opinion that we had done the country a service by showing how vulnerable we were to a panic reaction in event of war. From that time on the tide turned in our favor and, for better or worse, the course of all our lives was changed. The Mercury Theatre, whose brilliant production had brought about this explosive result, was soon to disband.

Orson, an instant world celebrity, transported the Mercury players to Hollywood and made the classic *Citizen Kane*. Joseph Cotten, one of the cast, achieved stardom while John Houseman produced several distinguished films and helped to establish the Stratford Shakespearean Theatre. As for me, I was catapulted to Hollywood and a seven-year contract at Warner Brothers.

At first the studio was at a loss how to use me. Accustomed to typecast writers as well as actors, they had no previous experience with Martians with whom they identified me. Finally I fell heir to some assorted scenes and scraps of dialogue written and then abandoned by two previous writers. I was told to construct a story incorporating these fragments for a production that was scheduled to start in two months. With the camera breathing down my neck I began writing in desperation with only the vaguest notion where each scene was leading, hoping that it would lead to another scene and another and that the sum total, if I lived that long, would add up to a film that wouldn't be bad enough to end my brief career in Hollywood.

Again as in the case of the Martian broadcast, I was the chance beneficiary of what seems like another miracle. By virtue of a production in which all the elements fused — Michael Curtiz, the director, and a superb cast headed by Humphrey Bogart and Ingrid Bergman — my patchwork script survived its chaotic birth and emerged as a film which has endured over the years, revitalized today by the young generation who apparently have adopted it as their own. The name of the film is *Casablanca*.

And what of the Martians, those formidable beings we let loose on the world that eventful night, finally laid low by bacteria, "the humblest thing that God in His wisdom put upon this earth"? We know more about conditions on Mars today than we did in 1938 but, even after the recent photographs sent back by Mariner, scientists are divided on the question whether or not some form of life exists on the planet. We can be quite certain, however, that there are no creatures there capable of invading the earth. The converse seems much more possible — that in the not-too-distant future we earthlings will be capable of invading Mars. And let any living creatures there take warning. We have destructive machines and toxic gases hardly less deadly than those H. G. Wells assigned to the Martians.

In the past several decades a controversy has arisen over the appearance in our skies of unidentified flying objects, popularly known as flying saucers because of their circular shape. Perhaps conditioned by our broadcast, those who first believed these objects to be extraterrestrial jumped to the conclusion that they came from Mars, a theory since dispelled in favor of some planet in another galaxy.

Imaginary or otherwise, sightings have been reported in various parts of the world, often by observers as qualified as scientists and airline pilots. In New Mexico, New Hampshire and Michigan hundreds of people living in those areas

— farmers, teachers, students, housewives, police officers — have seen these objects, some at fairly close range, and their descriptions of the size, shape, color and movement of the objects have been remarkably similar. Without claiming any personal knowledge, I find it difficult to believe that all these people have been playing games (hoaxes) or have suffered from optical illusions or some form of mass hysteria. Yet from the earliest sightings the United States air force has been at great pains to deny the existence of these flying objects. When under public pressure they have conducted or sponsored investigations, their research seemed to proceed from a predetermined premise that the objects did not exist and to disregard a great weight of evidence on the affirmative side.

No doubt the air force has its own reasons to play down the sightings. Possibly mindful of the panic caused by our Martian broadcast, they wanted to avoid a repetition. Understandably they are anxious to reassure us that nothing exists in this world which is not in their power to cope with. However, reassurances, too insistently reiterated, often have the opposite effect from the one intended. From interviews after the broadcast, we found that the pronouncements of the scientists, the military men and the Secretary of the Interior reassuring the listeners that everything was under control and there was no cause for alarm only succeeded in convincing them that the truth was being withheld and that the invaders were, indeed, Martians, invincible and bent on our destruction.

Among humans there appears to be a curious assumption that any visitor to our planet from outer space must have come with hostile intentions. Why? I think the answer lies in our own psyches. As a people we suffer from xenophobia, fear of anything alien, which accounts for many of our racial and national prejudices against those whose color or religion or economic system is different from ours. We tend to assign to others our own fears and aggressions. Hence it was natural for the Michigan farmer who believed he saw one of the objects hovering over a swamp on his land to run into his house for his shotgun instead of making some more hospitable gesture.

If our radio play had portrayed the Martians as arrivals on a friendly mission, I suspect our audience would have been less ready to accept the drama as something actually happening. Yet, as Arthur Clarke pointed out, why shouldn't creatures evolved enough to span the galaxies be intelligent enough to share a peaceful existence with other living beings? They may even help to save us from ourselves. I hope that, if a "saucer" ever lands on my property, I will have the sense to hold out my hand and invite its occupants in my house for a sandwich and a cup of coffee.

People have asked me whether I'd write another radio play of the kind that might contribute to some future panic. The answer is no. I have no desire to increase our xenophobia or to add to the very real alarms of our precarious times. I recall a story told me by a woman in a telephone exchange the night of the broadcast. She was supervising the girls who answer information calls. The company was just instituting a new policy to give the customers more courteous service. Walking down the row of switchboards, my informant heard one of the girls say in a very polite tone, "I'm sorry, we haven't that information here." The supervisor stopped to compliment her. "That was very nicely spoken. What did the party ask?" The girl replied, "He wanted to know if the world was coming to an end."

II

THE RADIO PLAY

"Incredible as it may seem . . ."

COLUMBIA BROADCASTING SYSTEM
ORSON WELLES AND MERCURY THEATRE
ON THE AIR
SUNDAY, OCTOBER 30, 1938
8:00 TO 9:00 P.M.

ANNOUNCER: The Columbia Broadcasting System and its affiliated stations present Orson Welles and the Mercury Theatre on the Air in a radio play by Howard Koch suggested by the H. G. Wells novel *The War of the Worlds*.

(*Mercury Theatre Musical Theme*)

ANNOUNCER: Ladies and gentlemen: the director of the Mercury Theatre and star of these broadcasts, Orson Welles . . .

ORSON WELLES

We know now that in the early years of the twentieth century this world was being watched closely by intelligences greater than man's and yet as mortal as his own. We know now that as human beings busied themselves about their various concerns they were scrutinized and studied, perhaps almost as narrowly as a man with a microscope might scrutinize the transient creatures that

The broadcast.

swarm and multiply in a drop of water. With infinite complacence people went to and fro over the earth about their little affairs, serene in the assurance of their dominion over this small spinning fragment of solar driftwood which by chance or design man has inherited out of the dark mystery of Time and Space. Yet across an immense ethereal gulf, minds that are to our minds as ours are to the beasts in the jungle, intellects vast, cool and unsympathetic, regarded this earth with envious eyes and slowly and surely drew their plans against us. In the thirty-eighth year of the twentieth century came the great disillusionment.

It was near the end of October. Business was better. The war was over. More men were back at work. Sales were picking up. On this particular evening, October 30, the Crossley service estimated that thirty-two million people were listening in on radios.

ANNOUNCER

. . . for the next twenty-four hours not much change in temperature. A slight atmospheric disturbance of undetermined origin is reported over Nova Scotia, causing a low pressure area to move down rather rapidly over the northeastern states, bringing a forecast of rain, accompanied by winds of light gale force. Maximum temperature 66; minimum 48. This weather report comes to you from the Government Weather Bureau.

. . . We now take you to the Meridian Room in

the Hotel Park Plaza in downtown New York, where you will be entertained by the music of Ramón Raquello and his orchestra.

(*Spanish theme song . . . fades*)

ANNOUNCER THREE

Good evening, ladies and gentlemen. From the Meridian Room in the Park Plaza in New York City, we bring you the music of Ramón Raquello and his orchestra. With a touch of the Spanish, Ramón Raquello leads off with "La Cumparsita."

(*Piece starts playing*)

ANNOUNCER TWO

Ladies and gentlemen, we interrupt our program of dance music to bring you a special bulletin from the Intercontinental Radio News. At twenty minutes before eight, central time, Professor Farrell of the Mount Jennings Observatory, Chicago, Illinois, reports observing several explosions of incandescent gas, occurring at regular intervals on the planet Mars.

The spectroscope indicates the gas to be hydrogen and moving towards the earth with enormous velocity. Professor Pierson of the observatory at Princeton confirms Farrell's observation, and describes the phenomenon as (quote) like a jet of blue flame shot from a gun (unquote). We now return you to the music of Ramón Raquello, playing for you in the Meridian Room of the Park Plaza Hotel, situated in downtown New York.

(Music plays for a few moments until piece ends . . . sound of applause)

Now a tune that never loses favor, the ever-popular "Star Dust." Ramón Raquello and his orchestra . . .

(Music)

ANNOUNCER TWO

Ladies and gentlemen, following on the news given in our bulletin a moment ago, the Government Meteorological Bureau has requested the large observatories of the country to keep an astronomical watch on any further disturbances occurring on the planet Mars. Due to the unusual nature of this occurrence, we have arranged an interview with the noted astronomer, Professor Pierson, who will give us his views on this event. In a few moments we will take you to the Princeton Observatory at Princeton, New Jersey. We return you until then to the music of Ramón Raquello and his orchestra.

(Music . . .)

ANNOUNCER TWO

We are ready now to take you to the Princeton Observatory at Princeton where Carl Phillips, our commentator, will interview Professor Richard Pierson, famous astronomer. We take you now to Princeton, New Jersey.

(Echo chamber)

PHILLIPS

Good evening, ladies and gentlemen. This is Carl Phillips, speaking to you from the observatory at Princeton. I am standing in a large semicircular room, pitch black except for an oblong split in the ceiling. Through this opening I can see a sprinkling of stars that cast a kind of frosty glow over the intricate mechanism of the huge telescope. The ticking sound you hear is the vibration of the clockwork. Professor Pierson stands directly above me on a small platform, peering through the giant lens. I ask you to be patient, ladies and gentlemen, during any delay that may arise during our interview. Beside his ceaseless watch of the heavens, Professor Pierson may be interrupted by telephone or other communications. During this period he is in constant touch with the astronomical centers of the world . . . Professor, may I begin our questions?

PIERSON

At any time, Mr. Phillips.

PHILLIPS

Professor, would you please tell our radio audience exactly what you see as you observe the planet Mars through your telescope?

PIERSON

Nothing unusual at the moment, Mr. Phillips. A red disk swimming in a blue sea. Transverse stripes across the disk. Quite distinct now because Mars happens to be at the point nearest the earth . . . in opposition, as we call it.

PHILLIPS

In your opinion, what do these transverse stripes signify, Professor Pierson?

PIERSON

Not canals, I can assure you, Mr. Phillips, although that's the popular conjecture of those who imagine Mars to be inhabited. From a scientific viewpoint the stripes are merely the result of atmospheric conditions peculiar to the planet.

PHILLIPS

Then you're quite convinced as a scientist that living intelligence as we know it does not exist on Mars?

PIERSON

I should say the chances against it are a thousand to one.

PHILLIPS

And yet how do you account for these gas eruptions occurring on the surface of the planet at regular intervals?

PIERSON

Mr. Phillips, I cannot account for it.

PHILLIPS

By the way, Professor, for the benefit of our listeners, how far is Mars from the earth?

PIERSON

Approximately forty million miles.

PHILLIPS

Well, that seems a safe enough distance.

PHILLIPS

Just a moment, ladies and gentlemen, someone has just handed Professor Pierson a message. While he reads it, let me remind you that we are speaking to you from the observatory in Princeton, New Jersey, where we are interviewing the world-famous astronomer, Professor Pierson . . . One moment, please. Professor Pierson has passed me a message which he has just received . . . Professor, may I read the message to the listening audience?

PIERSON

Certainly, Mr. Phillips.

PHILLIPS

Ladies and gentlemen, I shall read you a wire addressed to Professor Pierson from Dr. Gray of the National History Museum, New York. "9:15 P.M. eastern standard time. Seismograph registered shock of almost earthquake intensity occurring within a radius of twenty miles of Princeton. Please investigate. Signed, Lloyd Gray, Chief of Astronomical Division." . . . Professor Pierson, could this occurrence possibly have something to do with the disturbances observed on the planet Mars?

PIERSON

Hardly, Mr. Phillips. This is probably a meteorite of unusual size and its arrival at this particular time is merely a coincidence. However, we shall conduct a search, as soon as daylight permits.

PHILLIPS

Thank you, Professor. Ladies and gentlemen, for the past ten minutes we've been speaking to you from the observatory at Princeton, bringing you a special interview with Professor Pierson, noted astronomer. This is Carl Phillips speaking. We now return you to our New York studio.

(*Fade in piano playing*)

ANNOUNCER TWO

Ladies and gentlemen, here is the latest bulletin from the Intercontinental Radio News. Montreal, Canada: Professor Morse of McGill University reports observing a total of three explosions on the planet Mars, between the hours of 7:45 P.M. and 9:20 P.M., eastern standard time. This confirms earlier reports received from American observatories. Now, nearer home, comes a special announcement from Trenton, New Jersey. It is reported that at 8:50 P.M. a huge, flaming object, believed to be a meteorite, fell on a farm in the neighborhood of Grovers Mill, New Jersey, twenty-two miles from Trenton. The flash in the sky was visible within a radius of several hundred miles and the noise of the impact was heard as far north as Elizabeth.

We have dispatched a special mobile unit to the scene, and will have our commentator, Mr. Phillips, give you a word description as soon as he can reach there from Princeton. In the meantime, we take you to the Hotel Martinet in Brooklyn, where Bobby Millette and his orchestra are offering a program of dance music.

> (*Swing band for twenty seconds* . . .
> *then cut*)

ANNOUNCER TWO

We take you now to Grovers Mill, New Jersey.
> (*Crowd noises* . . . *police sirens*)

PHILLIPS

Ladies and gentlemen, this is Carl Phillips again, at the Wilmuth farm, Grovers Mill, New Jersey. Professor Pierson and myself made the eleven miles from Princeton in ten minutes. Well, I . . . I hardly know where to begin, to paint for you a word picture of the strange scene before my eyes, like something out of a modern *Arabian Nights*.

Well, I just got here. I haven't had a chance to look around yet. I guess that's it. Yes, I guess that's the . . . thing, directly in front of me, half buried in a vast pit. Must have struck with terrific force. The ground is covered with splinters of a tree it must have struck on its way down. What I can see of the . . . object itself doesn't look very much like a meteor, at least not the meteors I've seen. It looks more like a huge cylinder. It has a diameter of . . . what would you say, Professor Pierson?

PIERSON
(*Off*)

About thirty yards.

PHILLIPS

About thirty yards . . . The metal on the sheath is . . . well, I've never seen anything like it. The color is sort of yellowish-white. Curious spectators now are pressing close to the object in spite of the efforts of the police to keep them back. They're getting in front of my line of vision. Would you mind standing on one side, please?

POLICEMAN

One side, there, one side.

PHILLIPS

While the policemen are pushing the crowd back, here's Mr. Wilmuth, owner of the farm here.

He may have some interesting facts to add. . . . Mr. Wilmuth, would you please tell the radio audience as much as you remember of this rather unusual visitor that dropped in your backyard? Step closer, please. Ladies and gentlemen, this is Mr. Wilmuth.

WILMUTH

I was listenin' to the radio.

PHILLIPS

Closer and louder, please.

WILMUTH

Pardon me!

PHILLIPS

Louder, please, and closer.

WILMUTH

Yes, sir — while I was listening to the radio and kinda drowsin', that Professor fellow was talkin' about Mars, so I was half dozin' and half . . .

PHILLIPS

Yes, Mr. Wilmuth. Then what happened?

WILMUTH

As I was sayin', I was listenin' to the radio kinda halfways . . .

PHILLIPS

Yes, Mr. Wilmuth, and then you saw something?

WILMUTH

Not first off. I heard something.

PHILLIPS

And what did you hear?

WILMUTH

A hissing sound. Like this: sssssss . . . kinda like a fourt' of July rocket.

PHILLIPS

Then what?

WILMUTH

Turned my head out the window and would have swore I was to sleep and dreamin'.

PHILLIPS

Yes?

WILMUTH

I seen a kinda greenish streak and then zingo! Somethin' smacked the ground. Knocked me clear out of my chair!

PHILLIPS

Well, were you frightened, Mr. Wilmuth?

WILMUTH

Well, I — I ain't quite sure. I reckon I — I was kinda riled.

PHILLIPS

Thank you, Mr. Wilmuth. Thank you.

WILMUTH

Want me to tell you some more?

PHILLIPS

No . . . That's quite all right, that's plenty.

PHILLIPS

Ladies and gentlemen, you've just heard Mr. Wilmuth, owner of the farm where this thing has fallen. I wish I could convey the atmosphere . . . the background of this . . . fantastic scene. Hundreds of cars are parked in a field in back of us. Police are trying to rope off the roadway leading into the farm. But it's no use. They're breaking right through. Their headlights throw an enormous spot on the pit where the object's half buried. Some of the more daring souls are venturing near the edge. Their silhouettes stand out against the metal sheen.

(Faint humming sound)

One man wants to touch the thing . . . he's having an argument with a policeman. The policeman wins. . . . Now, ladies and gentlemen,

47

there's something I haven't mentioned in all this excitement, but it's becoming more distinct. Perhaps you've caught it already on your radio. Listen: (*Long pause*) . . . Do you hear it? It's a curious humming sound that seems to come from inside the object. I'll move the microphone nearer. Here. (*Pause*) Now we're not more than twenty-five feet away. Can you hear it now? Oh, Professor Pierson!

PIERSON

Yes, Mr. Phillips?

PHILLIPS

Can you tell us the meaning of that scraping noise inside the thing?

PIERSON

Possibly the unequal cooling of its surface.

PHILLIPS

Do you still think it's a meteor, Professor?

PIERSON

I don't know what to think. The metal casing is definitely extraterrestrial . . . not found on this earth. Friction with the earth's atmosphere usually tears holes in a meteorite. This thing is smooth and, as you can see, of cylindrical shape.

PHILLIPS

Just a minute! Something's happening! Ladies and gentlemen, this is terrific! This end of the thing is beginning to flake off! The top is beginning to rotate like a screw! The thing must be hollow!

VOICES

She's a movin'!
Look, the darn thing's unscrewing!
Keep back, there! Keep back, I tell you!
Maybe there's men in it trying to escape!
It's red hot, they'll burn to a cinder!
Keep back there. Keep those idiots back!
(*Suddenly the clanking sound of a huge piece of falling metal*)

VOICES

She's off! The top's loose!
Look out there! Stand back!

PHILLIPS

Ladies and gentlemen, this is the most terrifying thing I have ever witnessed . . . Wait a minute! *Someone's crawling out of the hollow top.* Someone or . . . something. I can see peering out of that black hole two luminous disks . . . are they eyes? It might be a face. It might be . . .
(*Shout of awe from the crowd*)

49

PHILLIPS

Good heavens, something's wriggling out of the shadow like a gray snake. Now it's another one, and another. They look like tentacles to me. There, I can see the thing's body. It's large as a bear and it glistens like wet leather. But that face. It . . . it's indescribable. I can hardly force myself to keep looking at it. The eyes are black and gleam like a serpent. The mouth is V-shaped with saliva dripping from its rimless lips that seem to quiver and pulsate. The monster or whatever it is can hardly move. It seems weighed down by . . . possibly gravity or something. The thing's raising up. The crowd falls back. They've seen enough. This is the most extraordinary experience. I can't find words . . . I'm pulling this microphone with me as I talk. I'll have to stop the description until I've taken a new position. Hold on, will you please, I'll be back in a minute.

(*Fade into piano*)

ANNOUNCER TWO

We are bringing you an eyewitness account of what's happening on the Wilmuth farm, Grovers Mill, New Jersey. (*More piano*) We now return you to Carl Phillips at Grovers Mill.

PHILLIPS

Ladies and gentlemen (Am I on?). Ladies and gentlemen, here I am, back of a stone wall that adjoins Mr. Wilmuth's garden. From here I get a sweep of the whole scene. I'll give you every detail as long as I can talk. As long as I can see. More state police have arrived. They're drawing up a cordon in front of the pit, about thirty of them. No need to push the crowd back now. They're willing to keep their distance. The captain is conferring with someone. We can't quite see who. Oh yes, I believe it's Professor Pierson. Yes, it is. Now they've parted. The professor moves around one side, studying the object, while the captain and two policemen advance with something in their hands. I can see it now. It's a white handkerchief tied to a pole . . . a flag of truce. If those creatures know what that means . . . what anything means! . . . *Wait!* Something's happening!

(*Hissing sound followed by a humming that increases in intensity*)

A humped shape is rising out of the pit. I can make out a small beam of light against a mirror. What's that? There's a jet of flame springing from that mirror, and it leaps right at the advancing men. It strikes them head on! Good Lord, they're turning into flame!

(*Screams and unearthly shrieks*)

Now the whole field's caught fire. (*Explosion*) The woods . . . the barns . . . the gas tanks of automobiles . . . it's spreading everywhere. It's coming this way. About twenty yards to my right . . .

(*Crash of microphone . . . then dead silence*)

ANNOUNCER TWO

Ladies and gentlemen, due to circumstances beyond our control, we are unable to continue the broadcast from Grovers Mill. Evidently there's some difficulty with our field transmission. However, we will return to that point at the earliest opportunity. In the meantime, we have a late bulletin from San Diego, California. Professor Indellkoffer, speaking at a dinner of the California Astronomical Society, expressed the opinion that the explosions on Mars are undoubtedly nothing more than severe volcanic disturbances on the surface of the planet. We continue now with our piano interlude.

(*Piano . . . then cut*)

Ladies and gentlemen, I have just been handed a message that came in from Grovers Mill by telephone. Just a moment. At least forty people, including six state troopers lie dead in a field east of the village of Grovers Mill, their bodies burned and distorted beyond all possible recognition. The next voice you hear will be that of Brigadier General Montgomery Smith, commander of the state militia at Trenton, New Jersey.

SMITH

I have been requested by the governor of New Jersey to place the counties of Mercer and Middle-

sex as far west as Princeton, and east to Jamesburg, under martial law. No one will be permitted
to enter this area except by special pass issued by
state or military authorities. Four companies of
state militia are proceeding from Trenton to Grovers Mill, and will aid in the evacuation of homes
within the range of military operations. Thank
you.

ANNOUNCER

You have just been listening to General Montgomery Smith, commanding the state militia at
Trenton. In the meantime, further details of the
catastrophe at Grovers Mill are coming in. The
strange creatures after unleashing their deadly
assault, crawled back in their pit and made no attempt to prevent the efforts of the firemen to re-
cover the bodies and extinguish the fire. Combined
fire departments of Mercer County are fighting the
flames which menace the entire countryside.

We have been unable to establish any contact
with our mobile unit at Grovers Mill, but we hope
to be able to return you there at the earliest possible moment. In the meantime we take you — uh,
just one moment please.

(*Long pause*)

(*Whisper*) Ladies and gentlemen, I have just
been informed that we have finally established
communication with an eyewitness of the tragedy.
Professor Pierson has been located at a farmhouse

53

near Grovers Mill where he has established an emergency observation post. As a scientist, he will give you his explanation of the calamity. The next voice you hear will be that of Professor Pierson, brought to you by direct wire. Professor Pierson.

PIERSON

Of the creatures in the rocket cylinder at Grovers Mill, I can give you no authoritative information — either as to their nature, their origin, or their purposes here on earth. Of their destructive instrument I might venture some conjectural explanation. For want of a better term, I shall refer to the mysterious weapon as a heat ray. It's all too evident that these creatures have scientific knowledge far in advance of our own. It is my guess that in some way they are able to generate an intense heat in a chamber of practically absolute nonconductivity. This intense heat they project in a parallel beam against any object they choose, by means of a polished parabolic mirror of unknown composition, much as the mirror of a lighthouse projects a beam of light. That is my conjecture of the origin of the heat ray . . .

ANNOUNCER TWO

Thank you, Professor Pierson. Ladies and gentlemen, here is a bulletin from Trenton. It is a brief statement informing us that the charred body of Carl Phillips has been identified in a Trenton hospital. Now here's another bulletin from Washington, D.C.

Office of the director of the National Red Cross reports ten units of Red Cross emergency workers have been assigned to the headquarters of the state militia stationed outside of Grovers Mill, New Jersey. Here's a bulletin from state police, Princeton Junction: The fires at Grovers Mill and vicinity now under control. Scouts report all quiet in the pit, and no sign of life appearing from the mouth of the cylinder . . . And now, ladies and gentlemen, we have a special statement from Mr. Harry McDonald, vice-president in charge of operations.

MC DONALD

We have received a request from the militia at Trenton to place at their disposal our entire broadcasting facilities. In view of the gravity of the situation, and believing that radio has a definite responsibility to serve in the public interest at all times, we are turning over our facilities to the state militia at Trenton.

ANNOUNCER

We take you now to the field headquarters of the state militia near Grovers Mill, New Jersey.

CAPTAIN

This is Captain Lansing of the signal corps, attached to the state militia now engaged in military operations in the vicinity of Grovers Mill. Situation arising from the reported presence of certain individuals of unidentified nature is now under complete control.

The cylindrical object which lies in a pit directly below our position is surrounded on all sides by eight battalions of infantry, without heavy field-pieces, but adequately armed with rifles and machine guns. All cause for alarm, if such cause ever existed, is now entirely unjustified. The things, whatever they are, do not even venture to poke their heads above the pit. I can see their hiding place plainly in the glare of the searchlights here. With all their reported resources, these creatures can scarcely stand up against heavy machine-gun fire. Anyway, it's an interesting outing for the troops. I can make out their khaki uniforms, crossing back and forth in front of the lights. It looks almost like a real war. There appears to be some slight smoke in the woods bordering the Millstone River. Probably fire started by campers. Well, we ought to see some action soon. One of the companies is deploying on the left flank. A quick thrust and it will all be over. Now wait a minute! I see something on top of the cylinder. No, it's nothing but a shadow. Now the troops are on the edge of the Wilmuth farm. Seven thousand armed men closing in on an old metal tube. Wait, that wasn't a shadow! It's something moving . . . solid metal . . . kind of a shieldlike affair rising up out of the cylinder . . . It's going higher and higher. Why, it's standing on legs . . . actually rearing up on a sort of metal framework. Now it's reaching above the trees and the searchlights are on it! Hold on!

ANNOUNCER TWO

Ladies and gentlemen, I have a grave announcement to make. Incredible as it may seem, both the observations of science and the evidence of our eyes lead to the inescapable assumption that those strange beings who landed in the Jersey farmlands tonight are the vanguard of an invading army from the planet Mars. The battle which took place tonight at Grovers Mill has ended in one of the most startling defeats ever suffered by an army in modern times; seven thousand men armed with rifles and machine guns pitted against a single fighting machine of the invaders from Mars. One hundred and twenty known survivors. The rest strewn over the battle area from Grovers Mill to Plainsboro crushed and trampled to death under the metal feet of the monster, or burned to cinders by its heat ray. The monster is now in control of the middle section of New Jersey and has effectively cut the state through its center. Communication lines are down from Pennsylvania to the Atlantic Ocean. Railroad tracks are torn and service from New York to Philadelphia discontinued except routing some of the trains through Allentown and Phoenixville. Highways to the north, south, and west are clogged with frantic human traffic. Police and army reserves are unable to control the mad flight. By morning the fugitives will have swelled Philadelphia, Camden and Trenton, it is estimated, to twice their normal population.

At this time martial law prevails throughout New Jersey and eastern Pennsylvania. We take you now to Washington for a special broadcast on the National Emergency . . . the Secretary of the Interior . . .

SECRETARY

Citizens of the nation: I shall not try to conceal the gravity of the situation that confronts the country, nor the concern of your government in protecting the lives and property of its people. However, I wish to impress upon you — private citizens and public officials, all of you — the urgent need of calm and resourceful action. Fortunately, this formidable enemy is still confined to a comparatively small area, and we may place our faith in the military forces to keep them there. In the meantime placing our faith in God we must continue the performance of our duties each and every one of us, so that we may confront this destructive adversary with a nation united, courageous, and consecrated to the preservation of human supremacy on this earth. I thank you.

ANNOUNCER

You have just heard the Secretary of the Interior speaking from Washington. Bulletins too numerous to read are piling up in the studio here. We are informed that the central portion of New Jersey is blacked out from radio communication due to the effect of the heat ray upon power lines and electrical equipment. Here is a special bulletin from New York. Cables received from English, French, German scientific bodies offering assistance. Astronomers report continued gas outbursts at regular intervals on planet Mars. Majority voice opinion that enemy will be reinforced by additional rocket machines. Attempts made to locate Professor Pierson of Princeton, who has observed Martians at close range. It is feared he was lost in recent battle. Langham Field, Virginia: Scouting planes report three Martian machines visible above treetops, moving north towards Somerville with population fleeing ahead of them. Heat ray not in use; although advancing at express-train speed, invaders pick their way carefully. They seem to be making conscious effort to avoid destruction of cities and countryside. However, they stop to uproot power lines, bridges, and railroad tracks. Their apparent objective is to crush resistance, paralyze communication, and disorganize human society.

Here is a bulletin from Basking Ridge, New Jersey: Coon hunters have stumbled on a second cylinder similar to the first embedded in the great swamp twenty miles south of Morristown. U.S. army fieldpieces are proceeding from Newark to blow up second invading unit before cylinder can be opened and the fighting machine rigged. They are taking up position in the — foothills of Watchung Mountains. Another bulletin from Langham

Field, Virginia: Scouting planes report enemy machines, now three in number, increasing speed northward kicking over houses and trees in their evident haste to form a conjunction with their allies south of Morristown. Machines also sighted by telephone operator east of Middlesex within ten miles of Plainfield. Here's a bulletin from Winston Field, Long Island: Fleet of army bombers carrying heavy explosives flying north in pursuit of enemy. Scouting planes act as guides. They keep speeding enemy in sight. Just a moment please. Ladies and gentlemen, we've run special wires to the artillery line in adjacent villages to give you direct reports in the zone of the advancing enemy. First we take you to the battery of the 22nd Field Artillery, located in the Watchung Mountains.

OFFICER

Range, thirty-two meters.

GUNNER

Thirty-two meters.

OFFICER

Projection, thirty-nine degrees.

GUNNER

Thirty-nine degrees.

OFFICER

Fire! (*Boom of heavy gun . . . pause*)

OBSERVER

One hundred and forty yards to the right, sir.

OFFICER

Shift range . . . thirty-one meters.

GUNNER

Thirty-one meters.

OFFICER

Projection . . . thirty-seven degrees.

GUNNER

Thirty-seven degrees.

OFFICER

Fire! (*Boom of heavy gun . . . pause*)

OBSERVER

A hit, sir! We got the tripod of one of them. They've stopped. The others are trying to repair it.

OFFICER

Quick, get the range! Shift thirty meters.

GUNNER

Thirty meters.

OFFICER

Projection . . . twenty-seven degrees.

GUNNER

Twenty-seven degrees.

OFFICER

Fire! (*Boom of heavy gun . . . pause*)

OBSERVER

Can't see the shell land, sir. They're letting off a smoke.

OFFICER

What is it?

OBSERVER

A black smoke, sir. Moving this way. Lying close to the ground. It's moving fast.

OFFICER

Put on gas masks. (*Pause*) Get ready to fire. Shift to twenty-four meters.

GUNNER

Twenty-four meters.

OFFICER

Projection, twenty-four degrees.

GUNNER

Twenty-four degrees.

OFFICER

Fire! (*Boom*)

OBSERVER

Still can't see, sir. The smoke's coming nearer.

OFFICER

Get the range. (*Coughs*)

OBSERVER

Twenty-three meters. (*Coughs*)

OFFICER

Twenty-three meters. (*Coughs*)

GUNNER

Twenty-three meters. (*Coughs*)

OBSERVER

Projection, twenty-two degrees. (*Coughing*)

OFFICER

Twenty-two degrees. (*Fade in coughing*)
(*Fading in . . . sound of airplane motor*)

COMMANDER

Army bombing plane, V-8-43, off Bayonne, New Jersey, Lieutenant Voght, commanding eight bombers. Reporting to Commander Fairfax, Langham Field . . . This is Voght, reporting to Commander Fairfax, Langham Field . . . Enemy tripod machines now in sight. Reinforced by three machines from the Morristown cylinder . . . Six altogether. One machine partially crippled. Believed hit by shell from army gun in Watchung Mountains. Guns now appear silent. A heavy black fog hanging close to the earth . . . of extreme density, nature unknown. No sign of heat ray. Enemy now turns east, crossing Passaic River into the Jersey marshes. Another straddles the Pulaski Skyway. Evident objective is New York City. They're pushing down a high tension power station. The machines are close together now, and we're ready to attack. Planes circling, ready to strike. A thousand yards and we'll be over the first — eight hundred yards . . . six hundred . . . four hundred . . . two hundred . . . There they go! The giant arm raised . . . Green flash! They're spraying us with flame! Two thousand feet. Engines are giving out. No chance to release bombs. Only one thing left . . . drop on them, plane and all. We're diving on the first one. Now the engine's gone! Eight . . .

OPERATOR ONE

This is Bayonne, New Jersey, calling Langham Field . . .

This is Bayonne, New Jersey, calling Langham Field . . .

Come in, please . . . Come in, please . . .

OPERATOR TWO

This is Langham Field . . . go ahead . . .

OPERATOR ONE

Eight army bombers in engagement with enemy tripod machines over Jersey flats. Engines incapacitated by heat ray. All crashed. One enemy machine destroyed. Enemy now discharging heavy black smoke in direction of —

OPERATOR THREE

This is Newark, New Jersey. . .
This is Newark, New Jersey. . .
Warning! Poisonous black smoke pouring in from Jersey marshes. Reaches South Street. Gas masks useless. Urge population to move into open spaces . . . automobiles use Routes 7, 23, 24 . . . Avoid congested areas. Smoke now spreading over Raymond Boulevard . . .

OPERATOR FOUR

2X2L . . . calling CQ . . .
2X2L . . . calling CQ . . .
2X2L . . . calling 8X3R . . .
Come in, please . . .

OPERATOR FIVE

This is 8X3R . . . coming back at 2X2L.

OPERATOR FOUR

How's reception? How's reception? K, please. Where are you, 8X3R?
What's the matter? Where are you?
(*Bells ringing over city gradually diminishing*)

65

ANNOUNCER

I'm speaking from the roof of Broadcasting Building, New York City. The bells you hear are ringing to warn the people to evacuate the city as the Martians approach. Estimated in last two hours three million people have moved out along the roads to the north, Hutchison River Parkway still kept open for motor traffic. Avoid bridges to Long Island . . . hopelessly jammed. All communication with Jersey shore closed ten minutes ago. No more defenses. Our army wiped out . . . artillery, air force, everything wiped out. This may be the last broadcast. We'll stay here to the end . . . People are holding service below us . . . in the cathedral.

(*Voices singing hymn*)

Now I look down the harbor. All manner of boats, overloaded with fleeing population, pulling out from docks.

(*Sound of boat whistles*)

Streets are all jammed. Noise in crowds like New Year's Eve in city. Wait a minute . . . Enemy now in sight above the Palisades. Five great machines. First one is crossing river. I can see it from here, wading the Hudson like a man wading through a brook . . . A bulletin's handed me . . . Martian cylinders are falling all over the country. One outside Buffalo, one in Chicago, St. Louis . . . seem to be timed and spaced. . . . Now the first machine reaches the shore. He stands watching, looking over the city. His steel, cowlish head is even with the skyscrapers. He waits for the others. They rise like a line of new towers on the city's west side . . . Now they're lifting their metal hands. This is the end now. Smoke comes out . . . black smoke, drifting over the city. People in the streets see it now. They're running towards the East River . . . thousands of them, dropping in like rats. Now the smoke's spreading faster. It's reached Times Square. People trying to run away from it, but it's no use. They're falling like flies. Now the smoke's crossing Sixth Avenue . . . Fifth Avenue . . . one hundred yards away . . . it's fifty feet . . .

OPERATOR FOUR

2X2L calling CQ . . .
2X2L calling CQ . . .
2X2L calling CQ . . . New York.
Isn't there anyone on the air?
Isn't there anyone . . .
2X2L —

ANNOUNCER

You are listening to a CBS presentation of Orson Welles and the Mercury Theatre on the Air in an original dramatization of *The War of the Worlds* by H. G. Wells. The performance will continue after a brief intermission.

This is the Columbia . . . Broadcasting System.

(Music)

PIERSON

As I set down these notes on paper, I'm obsessed by the thought that I may be the last living man on earth. I have been hiding in this empty house near Grovers Mill — a small island of daylight cut off by the black smoke from the rest of the world. All that happened before the arrival of these monstrous creatures in the world now seems part of another life . . . a life that has no continuity with the present, furtive existence of the lonely derelict who pencils these words on the back of some astronomical notes bearing the signature of Richard Pierson. I look down at my blackened hands, my torn shoes, my tattered clothes, and I try to connect them with a professor who lives at Princeton, and who on the night of October 30, glimpsed through his telescope an orange splash of light on a distant planet. My wife, my colleagues, my students, my books, my observatory, my . . . my world . . . where are they? Did they ever exist? Am I Richard Pierson? What day is it? Do days exist without calendars? Does time pass when there are no human hands left to wind the clocks? . . . In writing down my daily life I tell myself I shall preserve human history between the dark covers of this little book that was meant to record the movements of the stars . . . But to write I must live, and to live I must eat . . . I find moldy bread in the kitchen, and an orange not too spoiled to swallow. I keep watch at the window. From time to time I catch sight of a Martian above the black smoke.

The smoke still holds the house in its black coil . . . But at length there is a hissing sound and suddenly I see a Martian mounted on his machine, spraying the air with a jet of steam, as if to dissipate the smoke. I watch in a corner as his huge metal legs nearly brush against the house. Exhausted by terror, I fall asleep . . . It's morning. Sun streams in the window. The black cloud of gas has lifted, and the scorched meadows to the north look as though a black snowstorm has passed over them. I venture from the house. I make my way to a road. No traffic. Here and there a wrecked car, baggage overturned, a blackened skeleton. I push on north. For some reason I feel safer trailing these monsters than running away from them. And I keep a careful watch. I have seen the Martians feed. Should one of their machines appear over the top of trees, I am ready to fling myself flat on the earth. I come to a chestnut tree. October, chestnuts are ripe. I fill my pockets. I must keep alive. Two days I wander in a vague northerly direction through a desolate world. Finally I notice a living creature . . . a small red squirrel in a beech tree. I stare at him, and wonder. He stares back at me. I believe at that moment the animal and I shared the same emotion . . . the joy of finding another living being . . . I push on north. I find dead cows in a brackish field. Beyond, the charred ruins of a dairy. The silo remains standing guard over the waste land like a lighthouse deserted by the sea. Astride the silo perches a weathercock. The arrow points north.

Next day I came to a city vaguely familiar in its contours, yet its buildings strangely dwarfed and leveled off, as if a giant had sliced off its highest towers with a capricious sweep of his hand. I reached the outskirts. I found Newark, undemolished, but humbled by some whim of the advancing Martians. Presently, with an odd feeling of being watched, I caught sight of something crouching in a doorway. I made a step towards it, and it rose up and became a man — a man, armed with a large knife.

STRANGER

Stop . . . Where did you come from?

PIERSON

I come from . . . many places. A long time ago from Princeton.

STRANGER

Princeton, huh? That's near Grovers Mill!

PIERSON

Yes.

STRANGER

Grovers Mill . . . (*Laughs as at a great joke*) There's no food here. This is my country . . . all this end of town down to the river. There's only food for one . . . Which way are you going?

PIERSON

I don't know. I guess I'm looking for — for people.

STRANGER

(*Nervously*) What was that? Did you hear something just then?

PIERSON

Only a bird (*Marvels*) . . . A live bird!

STRANGER

You get to know that birds have shadows these days . . . Say, we're in the open here. Let's crawl into this doorway and talk.

PIERSON

Have you seen any Martians?

STRANGER

They've gone over to New York. At night the sky is alive with their lights. Just as if people were still living in it. By daylight you can't see them. Five days ago a couple of them carried something big across the flats from the airport. I believe they're learning how to fly.

PIERSON

Fly!

STRANGER

Yeah, fly.

PIERSON

Then it's all over with humanity. Stranger, there's still you and I. Two of us left.

STRANGER

They got themselves in solid; they wrecked the greatest country in the world. Those green stars, they're probably falling somewhere every night. They've only lost one machine. There isn't anything to do. We're done. We're licked.

PIERSON

Where were you? You're in a uniform.

STRANGER

What's left of it. I was in the militia — national guard . . . That's good! Wasn't any war any more than there's war between men and ants.

PIERSON

And we're edible ants. I found that out . . . What will they do to us?

STRANGER

I've thought it all out. Right now we're caught as we're wanted. The Martian only has to go a few miles to get a crowd on the run. But they won't keep doing that. They'll begin catching us systematic like — keeping the best and storing us in cages and things. They haven't begun on us yet!

PIERSON

Not begun!

STRANGER

Not begun. All that's happened so far is because we don't have sense enough to keep quiet . . . bothering them with guns and such stuff and losing our heads and rushing off in crowds. Now instead of our rushing around blind we've got to fix ourselves up according to the way things are now. Cities, nations, civilization, progress . . . done.

PIERSON

But if that's so, what is there to live for?

STRANGER

There won't be any more concerts for a million years or so, and no nice little dinners at restaurants. If it's amusement you're after, I guess the game's up.

PIERSON

And what is there left?

STRANGER

Life . . . that's what! I want to live. And so do you! We're not going to be exterminated. And I don't mean to be caught, either, and tamed, and fattened, and bred like an ox.

PIERSON

What are you going to do?

STRANGER

I'm going on . . . right under their feet. I gotta plan. We men as men are finished. We don't know enough. We gotta learn plenty before we've got a chance. And we've got to live and keep free while we learn. I've thought it all out, see.

PIERSON

Tell me the rest.

STRANGER

Well, it isn't all of us that are made for wild beasts, and that's what it's got to be. That's why I watched you. All these little office workers that used to live in these houses — they'd be no good. They haven't any stuff to 'em. They just used to run off to work. I've seen hundreds of 'em, running wild to catch their commuters' train in the morning for fear that they'd get canned if they didn't;

running back at night afraid they won't be in time for dinner. Lives insured and a little invested in case of accidents. And on Sundays, worried about the hereafter. The Martians will be a godsend for those guys. Nice roomy cages, good food, careful breeding, no worries. After a week or so chasing about the fields on empty stomachs they'll come and be glad to be caught.

PIERSON

You've thought it all out, haven't you?

STRANGER

You bet I have! And that isn't all. These Martians will make pets of some of them, train 'em to do tricks. Who knows? Get sentimental over the pet boy who grew up and had to be killed. And some, maybe, they'll train to hunt us.

PIERSON

No, that's impossible. No human being . . .

STRANGER

Yes they will. There's men who'll do it gladly. If one of them ever comes after me . . .

PIERSON

In the meantime, you and I and others like us . . . where are we to live when the Martians own the earth?

STRANGER

I've got it all figured out. We'll live underground. I've been thinking about the sewers. Under New York are miles and miles of 'em. The main ones are big enough for anybody. Then there's cellars, vaults, underground storerooms, railway tunnels, subways. You begin to see, eh? And we'll get a bunch of strong men together. No weak ones, that rubbish, out.

PIERSON

And you meant me to go?

STRANGER

Well, I gave you a chance didn't I?

PIERSON

We won't quarrel about that. Go on.

STRANGER

And we've got to make safe places for us to stay in, see, and get all the books we can — science books. That's where men like you come in, see? We'll raid the museums, we'll even spy on the Martians. It may not be so much we have to learn before — just imagine this: four or five of their own fighting machines suddenly start off — heat rays right and left and not a Martian in 'em. Not a Martian in 'em! But *men* — men who have learned the way how. It may even be in our time. Gee! Imagine having one of them lovely things with its heat ray wide and free! We'd turn it on Martians, we'd turn it on men. We'd bring everybody down to their knees.

PIERSON

That's your plan?

STRANGER

You and me and a few more of us we'd own the world.

PIERSON

I see.

STRANGER

Say, what's the matter? Where are you going?

PIERSON

Not to your world . . . Good-bye, stranger . . .

PIERSON

After parting with the artilleryman, I came at last to the Holland Tunnel. I entered that silent tube anxious to know the fate of the great city on the other side of the Hudson. Cautiously I came out of the tunnel and made my way up Canal Street.

I reached Fourteenth Street, and there again were black powder and several bodies, and an evil ominous smell from the gratings of the cellars of some of the houses. I wandered up through the

Thirties and Forties; I stood alone on Times Square. I caught sight of a lean dog running down Seventh Avenue with a piece of dark brown meat in his jaws, and a pack of starving mongrels at his heels. He made a wide circle around me, as though he feared I might prove a fresh competitor. I walked up Broadway in the direction of that strange powder — past silent shopwindows, displaying their mute wares to empty sidewalks — past the Capitol Theatre, silent, dark — past a shooting gallery, where a row of empty guns faced an arrested line of wooden ducks. Near Columbus Circle I noticed models of 1939 motorcars in the showrooms facing empty streets. From over the top of the General Motors Building, I watched a flock of black birds circling in the sky. I hurried on. Suddenly I caught sight of the hood of a Martian machine, standing somewhere in Central Park, gleaming in the late afternoon sun. An insane idea! I rushed recklessly across Columbus Circle and into the Park. I climbed a small hill above the pond at Sixtieth Street. From there I could see, standing in a silent row along the mall, nineteen of those great metal Titans, their cowls empty, their steel arms hanging listlessly by their sides. I looked in vain for the monsters that inhabit those machines.

Suddenly, my eyes were attracted to the immense flock of black birds that hovered directly below me. They circled to the ground, and there before my eyes, stark and silent, lay the Martians, with the hungry birds pecking and tearing brown shreds of flesh from their dead bodies. Later when their bodies were examined in laboratories, it was found that they were killed by the putrefactive and disease bacteria against which their systems were unprepared . . . slain, after all man's defenses had failed, by the humblest thing that God in His wisdom put upon this earth.

Before the cylinder fell there was a general persuasion that through all the deep of space no life existed beyond the petty surface of our minute sphere. Now we see further. Dim and wonderful is the vision I have conjured up in my mind of life spreading slowly from this little seedbed of the solar system throughout the inanimate vastness of sidereal space. But that is a remote dream. It may be that the destruction of the Martians is only a reprieve. To them, and not to us, is the future ordained perhaps.

Strange it now seems to sit in my peaceful study at Princeton writing down this last chapter of the record begun at a deserted farm in Grovers Mill. Strange to see from my window the university spires dim and blue through an April haze. Strange to watch children playing in the streets. Strange to see young people strolling on the green, where the new spring grass heals the last black scars of a bruised earth. Strange to watch the sightseers enter the museum where the dissembled parts of a Martian machine are kept on public view. Strange when I recall the time when I first saw it, bright and clean-cut, hard and silent, under the dawn of that last great day.

(*Music*)

This is Orson Welles, ladies and gentlemen, out of character to assure you that The War of the Worlds has no further significance than as the holiday offering it was intended to be. The Mercury Theatre's own radio version of dressing up in a sheet and jumping out of a bush and saying Boo! Starting now, we couldn't soap all your windows and steal all your garden gates, by tomorrow night . . . so we did the next best thing. We annihilated the world before your very ears, and utterly destroyed the Columbia Broadcasting System. You will be relieved, I hope, to learn that we didn't mean it, and that both institutions are still open for business. So good-bye everybody, and remember, please, for the next day or so, the terrible lesson you learned tonight. That grinning, glowing, globular invader of your living room is an inhabitant of the pumpkin patch, and if your doorbell rings and nobody's there, that was no Martian . . . it's Hallowe'en.

III

THE AFTERMATH

"I thought it was all up with us."

"The panic came in the night. Here, there and everywhere people suddenly dropped to their knees and began to moan and babble. Housewives wept, tore their hair and fell into swoons. Grown men wept, too, and dashed about the streets. College boys trembled and prayed. Telephone lines were clogged with calls. In a few hours more the Red Cross and the National Guard would have had to be mobilized."

For days following the Martian broadcast headlines screamed and newspapers around the world tried to recreate the atmosphere of terror that spread over America on that October night. Even some years later the event is vividly recalled by an editor of the *New York Times* in the words quoted above.

During and after the broadcast frantic telephone calls flooded the switchboards of radio stations, newspapers and police headquarters. Some radio

"I had no idea . . ."

stations reported increases as much as five hundred percent over the usual Sunday night volume. Naturally it was CBS that received the full impact. I was not at the studio during the broadcast but John Houseman, co-producer of the show, was there and gives the following eyewitness account:

"At the height of the crisis, around 8:31 the Secretary of the Interior came on the air with an exhortation to the American people. Toward the end of this speech (circa 8:32 E.S.T.) Davidson Taylor, supervisor of the broadcast for the Columbia Broadcasting System, received a phone call in the control room, creased his lips, and hurriedly left the studio. By the time he returned a few moments later — pale as death — clouds of heavy smoke were rising from Newark, New Jersey, and the Martians, tall as skyscrapers, were astride the Pulaski Skyway preparatory to wading the Hudson River. To us in the studio, the show seemed to be progressing splendidly — how splendidly Davidson Taylor had just learned outside. For several minutes now a kind of madness had seemed to be sweeping the continent — somehow connected with our show. The CBS switchboards had been swamped into uselessness but from outside sources vague rumors were coming in of deaths and suicides and panic injuries. . . . I remember during the playing of the final theme, the phone started to ring in the control room and a shrill voice through the receiver announcing itself as the mayor of

some Midwestern city, one of the big ones. He is screaming for Welles. Choking with fury, he reports mobs in the streets of the city, women and children huddled in churches, violence and looting . . . Orson hangs up quickly. For we are now off the air and the studio door bursts open. The following hours are a nightmare. The building is suddenly full of people and dark blue uniforms. We are hurried out of the studio, downstairs, into a back office. Here we sit, incommunicado, while network employees are busily collecting, destroying or locking up all scripts and records of the broadcast. . . . Hours later, instead of arresting us, they let us out a back way. We scurry down to the theatre like hunted animals to their holes. It is surprising to see life going on as usual in the midnight streets."

The brunt of the public outcry fell on Orson. For days he was pursued by reporters and threatened by outraged citizens. Law suits for injuries and damages were filed against CBS and Mercury Theatre, running into millions of dollars, but none of these came to trial since there was no applicable precedent for such actions under those circumstances. As the shock was absorbed and the excitement died down, the tide of public opinion reversed itself. Mail continued to pour into radio stations but the vast majority were favorable, even congratulatory. Stories of individual experiences during the panic are recounted to this day like the

The brunt of the public outcry fell on Orson.

reminiscences of people who have lived through an actual war.

"I tuned in when the weather reports were given. I was with my little boy. My husband was at the movies. I thought it was all up with us. I grabbed my boy and just sat and cried."

This reaction of a mother living in a crowded New Jersey tenement was typical of many in several important respects. She saw certain death facing not only herself and her family but the "us" included the whole human race. It was tragedy on an incomprehensible scale. Over aeons of time man had survived the long and perilous climb from his sea origins through the jungles to a relatively civilized state. Having gained dominion over the earth, he was beginning to dream of reaching other planets. In one night his illusions of mastery were shattered. Creatures infinitely more advanced in technology were arriving from the reddish-hued planet his ancestors had named for the god of war and these formidable strangers were taking over the earth. Little wonder that this woman "sat down and cried."

But first she grabbed her little boy — another typical reaction. Few people want to live alone; no one wants to die alone. Holding the hand of someone we know and trust — relative, friend, priest or doctor — we are better able to face the unknown. Only at a moment of extremity do we realize how closely our lives are intertwined with others whom we normally take for granted.

After the broadcast almost everyone I met had a story to tell, either a personal experience or something that happened to someone he knew. Many of these accounts told of frantic efforts to reach absent members of their family before the end came. The head of the location department at Warner Brothers studio told me his experience in these words as nearly as I can recall them:

"My wife and I were driving through the redwood forest in northern California when the broadcast came over our car radio. At first it was just New Jersey but soon the things were landing all over, even in California. There was no escape. All we could think of was to try to get back to L.A. to see our children once more. And be with them when it happened. We went right by gas stations but I forgot we were low in gas. In the middle of the forest our gas ran out. There was nothing to do. We just sat there holding hands expecting any minute to see those Martian monsters appear over the tops of the trees. When Orson said it was a Hallowe'en prank, it was like being reprieved on the way to the gas chamber."

Some of the stories had their humorous aspect — at least in retrospect. This account came from a young college student:

"Mars Panic" Useful *By Hugh S. Johnson*

WASHINGTON, Nov. 2.—One of the most remarkable demonstrations of modern times was the startling effect of the absurd radio scenario of Orson Welles based on an old Jules Verne type of novel by H. G. Wells—"The War of the Worlds."

Simulated Columbia broadcast radio flashes of a pretended attack, with mysterious new aerial weapons, on New Jersey from the planet Mars, put many people into such a panic that the witch-burning Mr. McNinch, chairman of the Federal Communications Commission, has a new excuse to extend the creeping hand of government restriction of free speech by way of radio censorship.

When the hysterical echoes of an initial hysterical explosion die down the whole incident will assay out as about the silliest teapot tempest in human history.

There are no men on Mars. If there were there would be no occasion for their attack on earth. If there were such an occasion there is no reason to believe that in Mars, or anywhere else, there are weapons that could devastate a State or two in fifteen minutes. The result of public panic was so absurd as to be unpredictable by anybody—even the Columbia Broadcasting System and the author of the script. The idea of using the incident to discipline or censor anybody is ridiculous.

Incident Significan...

But the incident is highly significant. It reveals dramatically a state of public mind. Too many people have been led by outright propaganda to believe in some new and magic power of air attack and other developments in the weapons of war.

It is true that they are far more powerful than they formerly were. But it is also true that the defensive weapons against them are also far more powerful. Thus it has always been since the days of the Macedonian phalanx. Always the dope is that some mad new armament is going to change the face of wa Always events prove that invention for defense keep abreast of invention for attack. Always it turns ou that the outcome is decided by the shock of masses men breast to breast—and in no other way.

This does not for a moment mean that this count. can neglect any development of its weapons for d fense. It has done that in the past. If this hysteric happening means anything it is that there is a vag restless suspicion among the people of the truth th there has been such neglect.

Many things have happened and—let us hope— time, to wake us up to these defensive defaults. The was the Munich sell-out and the sudden disclosure Hitler and Mussolini as masters of Europe through th neglect of their defenses by both England and Fran compared with the vast military preparations of th dictatorships. There are the slow leaks of some of th shocking things that Hitler suggested as his price fo peace, among them German air and naval bases the Caribbean—direct threats against us. Finall there comes this dramatic proof of the jitters of ou own people on the subject of our own defenses.

Aid to Defense Program.

On the face of things a similar thing will not b permitted to happen again by any of our great broa casting systems. But when the smoke all drifts aw their innocence will be clear and the value of th incident may be credited to them as unintended assis ance to the President's great defense program.

The crumbling of British and French power in E rope. Africa, the Atlantic and the Mediterranean, pl German aggressiveness and insistence on air and nav bases far too close to us for comfort, puts an entire new face on the defense program. If this nutty, pa icky development serves no other purpose than to mak that clearer, it will have served its unintended purpo and have proved its unpredictable value.

Copyright, 1938, by United Feature Syndicate, Inc.

RADIO   SCREEN   STAGE

VARIETY

PRICE 25c

Published Weekly at 154 West 46th Street, New York, N. Y., by Variety, Inc. Annual subscription, $10. Single copies, 25 cents.
Entered as second-class matter December 22, 1905, at the Post Office at New York, N. Y., under the Act of March 3, 1879.
COPYRIGHT 1938, BY VARIETY, INC. ALL RIGHTS RESERVED.

64 PAGES

Vol. 132. No. 8   NEW YORK, WEDNESDAY, NOVEMBER 2, 1938

RADIO DOES U. S. A FAVOR

It Seems to Me

By Heywood Broun

I'm still scared. I didn't hear the broadcast, and I doubt that I would have called up the police to complain merely because I heard that men from a strange machine were knocking the daylights out of Princeton. That doesn't happen to be news this season. My first reaction would have been, "That's no Martian but merely McDonald, of Harvard, carrying the ball on what the coaches call a 'naked reverse' or Sally Rand shift."

Just the same, I live in terror that almost any time now a metal cylinder will come to earth, and out of it will step fearsome creatures carrying death ray guns. And their faces will be forbidding, because the next radio invasion is likely to be an expedition of the censors.

Obviously, Orson Welles put too much curdle on the radio ways, but there isn't a chance on earth that any chain will sanction such a stunt again. In fact, I think it would be an excellent rule to make the provision that nothing can be put forward as a news broadcast unless it actually is news. This is a domain which should not be disturbed even for innocuous and comic effect. Nor do I think it would smack of censorship if plugs for a product were required to be identified as advertising matter.

Some of the entertainers and commentators have grown far too kittenish in slinging the cigarets and the tooth paste around in portions of the program theoretically devoted to comic relief. In spite of gooners such as the recent escapade about Mars, the radio remains inhibited and too timid for its own good.

* * *

Weapons More Devastating.

We have much more reason to fear censors than octopi from the distant skies. The weapons which they may use can be much more far-reaching and devastating than any to be conjured up in a fantastic horror story. It is not a good thing that thousands of gullible people should be needlessly frightened out of their wits, if any. Possibly it is too much to ask the mixed audiences which radio commands to face the inventions of that lively pseudo-scientific sort to which the imagination of H. G. Wells turned when he was very young.

But Mr. Wells, of late, has faced more factual subjects. I have not recently caught up with his current economic and political views, for he sets them down on paper at a pace which leaves the willing reader breathless. When last my eye encountered his words he was liberal rather than radical. But he possessed so lively a concern for the world and so deep a faith that it can be changed for the better that there is no telling what theory he may spring suddenly.

Up to last Sunday night the State Department seemed to be unruffled as to visits from Martians. There is no record that any stranger from that inhabited planet had ever been detained at Ellis Island for questioning or had his visa canceled. Of course, the line of questioning would be obvious.

* * *

Maybe a Socialist State.

According to such astronomy as I have picked up from the Sunday papers, Mars is noted for its canals. At certain seasons of the year a vast network of waterways seems to have been laid out upon its surface. The engineering feat appears so prodigious that there may be reason to suspect that it could be a co-operative enterprise undertaken by a Socialist state. It could even be Communistic.

To our discomfiture, American officials put no barriers in the way of military men from Mars. Their scientists and philosophers would hardly fare as well. In fact, I missed Orson Welles on Sunday because I was talking to John Strachey, an economist who happens to be a citizen of that same planet of which we are a part.

It is his intention to lecture at American colleges, but he has not yet won legal admission and remains bound to silence on a temporary parole from Ellis Island. He came in a ship and not a cylinder and carries no death ray gun, but there are those to whom his presence strikes terror. They fear words and ideas, although there is a cherished American belief that these are the staples by which free men live. And so I say again that we have far more to fear from the silhouette of the censor than from the shadow of Orson Welles.

ON THE RECORD

By DOROTHY THOMPSON

ALL unwittingly Mr. Orson Welles and the Mercury Theater of the Air have made one of the most fascinating and important demonstrations of all time. They have proved that a few effective voices, accompanied by sound effects, can so convince masses of people of a totally unreasonable, completely fantastic proposition as to create nation-wide panic.

They have demonstrated more potently than any argument, demonstrated beyond question of a doubt, the appalling dangers and enormous effectiveness of popular and theatrical demagoguery.

They have cast a brilliant and cruel light upon the failure of popular education.

They have shown up the incredible stupidity, lack of nerve and ignorance of thousands.

They have proved how easy it is to start a mass delusion.

They have uncovered the primeval fears lying under the thinnest surface of the so-called civilized man.

They have shown that man, when the victim of his own gullibility, turns to the government to protect him against his own errors of judgment.

The newspapers are correct in playing up this story over every other news event in the world. It is the story of the century.

And far from blaming Mr. Orson Welles, he ought to be given a Congressional medal and a national prize for having made the most amazing and important of contributions to the social sciences. For Mr. Orson Welles and his theater have made a greater contribution to an understanding of Hitlerism, Mussolinism, Stalinism, anti-Semitism and all the other terrorisms of our times than all the words about them that have been written by reasonable men. They have made the reductio ad absurdum of mass manias. They have thrown more light on recent events in Europe leading to the Munich pact than everything that has been said on the subject by all the journalists and commentators.

Hitler managed to scare all Europe to its knees a month ago, but he at least had an army and an air force to back up his shrieking words.

But Mr. Welles scared thousands into demoralization with nothing at all.

That historic hour on the air was an act of unconscious genius, performed by the very innocence of intelligence.

*   *   *

Nothing whatever about the dramatization of the "War of the Worlds" was in the least credible, no matter at what point the hearer might have tuned in. The entire verisimilitude was in the names of a few specific places. Monsters were depicted of a type that nobody has ever seen, equipped with "rays" entirely fantastic; they were described as "straddling the Pulaski Skyway," and throughout the broadcast they were referred to as Martians, men from another planet.

A twist of the dial would have established for anybody that the national catastrope was not being noted on any other station. A second of logic would have dispelled any terror. A notice that the broadcast came from a non-existent agency would have awakened skepticism.

A reference to the radio program would have established that the "War of the Worlds" was announced in advance.

The time element was obviously lunatic.

Listeners were told that "within two hours three million people had moved out of New York"—an obvious impossibility for the most disciplined army moving exactly

Mr. Welles and Mass Delusion

nned, and a double fallacy be-
se, only a few minutes before,
news of the arrival of the mon-
had been announced.

nd of course it was not even a
nned hoax. Nobody was more
prised at the result than Mr.
lles. The public was told at the
inning, at the end and during
course of the drama that it *was*
rama.

ut eyewitnesses presented them-
ves; the report became second
nd, third hand, fourth hand, and
ame more and more credible, so
t nurses and doctors and Na-
nal Guardsmen rushed to de-
se.

When the truth became known
reaction was also significant. The
eived were furious and of course
nanded that the state protect
m, demonstrating that they were
apable of relying on their own
gment.

gain there was a complete fail-
of logic. For if the deceived had
ught about it they would realize
t the greatest organizers of mass
terias and mass delusions today
states using the radio to excite
rors, incite hatreds, inflame
sses, win mass support for policies,
ate idolatries, abolish reason and
intain themselves in power.

he immediate moral is apparent
the whole incident is viewed in
son: no political body must ever,
er any circumstances, obtain a
nopoly of radio.

he second moral is that our pop-
r and universal education is fail-
to train reason and logic, even
the educated.

he third is that the populariza-
n of science has led to gullibility
d new superstitions, rather than
skepticism and the really scien-
c attitude of mind.

he fourth is that the power of
ss suggestion is the most potent
ce today and that the political

demagogue is more powerful than
all the economic forces.

For, mind you, Mr. Welles was
managing an obscure program, com-
peting with one of the most popular
entertainments on the air!

The conclusion is that the radio
must not be used to create mass
prejudices and mass divisions and
schisms, either by private individuals or by government or its agen-
cies, or its officials, or its opponents.

If people can be frightened out
of their wits by mythical men from
Mars, they can be frightened into
fanaticism by the fear of Reds,
or convinced that America is in the
hands of sixty families, or aroused
to revenge against any minority, or
terrorized into subservience to lead-
ership because of any imaginable
menace.

* * *

The technique of modern mass
politics calling itself democracy is
to create a fear—a fear of economic
royalists, or of Reds, or of Jews, or
of starvation, or of an outside
enemy—and exploit that fear into
obtaining subservience in return for
protection.

I wrote in this column a short
time ago that the new warfare was
waged by propaganda, the outcome
depending on which side could first
frighten the other to death.

The British people were frightened into obedience to a policy a
few weeks ago by a radio speech
and by digging a few trenches in
Hyde Park, and afterward led to
hysterical jubiliation over a catastrophic defeat for their democracy.

But Mr. Welles went all the politicians one better. He made the
scare to end scares, the menace to
end menaces, the unreason to end
unreason, the perfect demonstration
that the danger is not from Mars
but from the theatrical demagogue.

PREPAREDNESS VS. PANIC ISSUE

Strategists Taking Cognizance of That Sunday Night Broadcast—Dramatizes Vividly the Lack of Common Sense Should a Real Air Attack Ever Occur—Anti-Radio Press Overplayed It, for Its Own Reasons

ELLIOTT'S ANGLES

Near-hysteria broke out all over the United States Sunday (30) night as result of a fanciful invasion-from-Mars story by H. G. Wells which was broadcast over the Columbia Broadcasting System in the form of news flasher' One immediate effect of the strange behavior of the populace was to focus attention on various social and military implications.

tioned outside every obscure seaport. In the Spanish-American war before wireless) the lack of knowledge of the whereabouts of the Spanish admiral, Cervera, created an Atlantic seaboard panic. Political pressure kept Admiral Schley idle at Hampton Roads instead of sailing to join the American fleet in the West Indies. Panic was finally allayed by rigging up old (and useless) Civil War monitors and anchoring them all along the coast with naval reservists aboard.

It's 'the hysterical throb' in announcers' voices, the emotional reaction to isolated individual cases) wrought-up eye-witnesses, that must be feared from radio, he holds. But Major Elliott stresses that censorship is not desirable in a democracy, where full, unvarnished reports should be given the public, especially in war time, when rumors fly thick and fast, anyhow. It is especially then that a maximum of official information helps offset and neutralize unofficial whispers.

Waves of panic are commonplace. They usually are quickly brought under control, the major points usual. There is danger, however, of political pressure impeding strategy. Exaggerated tales of Germany having 10,000 planes panicked England and France, whereas the cold facts were that Germany has not over 3,000 planes. Radio can spread and radio can control ideas and information essential to national defense.

It is thought that the whole episode which has received enormous front page publicity by a radio-hat-

dropping the play-within-a-play technique of dramatic presentation. Orson Welles in his own right expressed bewilderment at the reaction and thought that fully adequate safeguards had been taken and that frequent mentions of Mars, death-rays and the other familiar abracadabra of weird fiction certainly made it clear.

CBS Statement

Columbia issued the following official statement:

'The Columbia Broadcasting System regrets that some listeners to the Orson Welles' Mercury Theatre on the Air program last night mistook fantasy for fact.

Announcements were made before, after and twice during the hour that we were presenting a dramatized version of the H. G. Wells fictional novel of the invasion of this world by the planet Mars. Further announcements that the whole incident was fiction were put on the network when telephone calls showed some listeners that failed to realize that they were hearing a play.

'In order that this may not happen again, the Program Department hereafter will not use the technique of a simulated news broadcast within a dramatization when the circumstances of the broadcast could cause immediate alarm to numbers of listeners.'

No Names and Addresses

Washington, Nov. 1.

Few minor tragedies were blamed

highest degree our obligation to the public.'

Nameless Would-Be Suicide

Pittsburgh, Nov. 1.

Unbelievable scenes took place locally, according to newspaper reports. One man (not named) told scribes that upon returning to his home, he found his wife in the bathroom with a bottle of poison in her hands, screaming 'I'd rather die this way than like that.'

Leaders in every walk of life here later called WJAS and newspaper offices and denounced the program as a 'hoax.'

Incredible Coincidence

Seattle, Nov. 1.

Women fainted and men prepared to take their families into the mountains for safe keeping when electric power failed at Concrete, nearby town of 1,000, during the radio program of Orson Welles Sunday night. Just at dramatic point in broadcast reported lights went out in most homes of that town. For a time the village verged on mass hysteria because of power failure many persons thought imaginary Martian invasion had reached Washington State.

Elsewhere in Northwest calls poured into newspapers, press and radio bureaus by thousands. In Seattle police station switchboards blanket of white lights from incoming calls from listeners who thought they were hearing bonafide news broadcast. Calls from as far as 200 ment expressed the view that besides revealing a jumpy state of nerves, brought on by the war clouds over Europe and Asia, the episode drove home how little prepared the nation is to cope with an abrupt emergency.

Thus, it is being pointed out, Columbia Broadcasting has inadvertently done a lot for national defense. It's also being said that the fantasy would have understood the fantasy if their parents hadn't gone off the deep end. (Paradoxically CBS has been a pioneer in barring kid programs of the cliffhanger kind from the air.)

What struck home on the social-military side represented (in its fictional situation) the American Secretary of the Interior as coming on the radio to urge calm and orderly action and saying further that the United States Army was coping with the imaginary emergency. Coincidental with this part of the broadcast story, enough people all over America were doing an aspenleaf act to present a spectacle probably without parallel.

A War Officer Speaks

Major George Fielding Elliott, army strategist and author of 'The Ramparts We Watch' (Reynal-Hitchcock), points out to VARIETY that panic by the populace is always one of the unpredictables of military and naval planning. During the Civil War delegations constantly plagued Washington to have naval vessels sta-

industry. This remains true even though the incident will undoubtedly be lovingly embraced by those who, consciously or unconsciously, want censorship.

That a sustaining program is capable of making an impact (no matter how) on the entire nation is further proof of the role radio plays in American family life.

CBS Not As Concerned

Columbia itself did not take the situation as seriously as the newspapers. It was particularly noticed that several dailies with axes to grind or grouches to nurse, where radio or the FCC were concerned, were leaders in laying it on and rubbing it in.

For years radio has broadcast fantastic stories of the kind that caused Sunday night's panic. Notably 'Buck Rogers in the 25th Century,' plus others. Two factors, however, must be added in accounting for Sunday's unpredictable reaction which was more incredible than the incredible H. G. Welles fiction story itself. First, the state of the world and the willingness to credit any sudden aggression gave force to the wild rumors that followed a careless listening of the show. Second, CBS employed the 'flash'! type of news bulletin which has been so common lately that its use as a dramatic device fell into well-rutted mental paths and was taken, unverified, as literal and not fictional.

Columbia early Monday announced that it was adopting a policy of

home from the hospital (unnamed) who was just ... (unnamed) and pulled the stitches closing her appendicitis scar or the man (unnamed) at Quantico, Va, who drove to Red Cross headquarters (where not stated) to find out where he and his family would be safe.

Flood of telephone calls to WJSV, local CBS outlet, swamped the telephone company. Station operators handled 500 calls, while the telephone company reported 12,000 individual attempts were made to get the transmitter during the excitement. All newspapers received scores of inquiries.

Realistic effect of the program on local dial-twisters was best illustrated by concern which prompted two grocery company executives (not identified) to make inquiries about sending food for the 'victims' of the planetary attack.

Neville Miller's Statement

Statement of Neville Miller, president of National Association of Broadcasters, on the H. G. Wells panic was:

'I know that the Columbia Broadcasting System and those of us in radio have only the most profound regret that the composure of many of our fellow citizens was disturbed last night by the vivid Orson Welles broadcast.

The Columbia Broadcasting System has taken immediate steps to insure that such program technique will not be used again. This instance emphasizes the responsibility we assume in the use of radio and renews our determination to fulfill to the

St. Louis, Nov. 1.

Hysteria bordering on panic was manifested here and in the local area during the broadcast of H. G. Wells' imaginary skit Sunday (30). Southwestern Bell Telephone Co's lines were jammed with calls from the East for 30 mins. After the broadcast CBS outlet, was swamped at KMOX, 700 calls, 25 of which were long distance.

Four announcements that the program was the 'Mercury theatre on the air' did not allay fear. Some women hired taxicabs to call for children, others behaved equally upset.

At the Strand theatre in St. Charles, Mo., a woman rushed into the house gathered up her children and took them home.

Police queried by phone for advice of the impending disaster and even assurances given that the broadcast was purely fictional did not completely dispel the mood engendered by the skit.

DuPonts Sponsoring?

Panic caused by Orson Welles' CBS broadcast of the 'War of Worlds' inspired one radio wag to observe:

The Mercury theatre will probably be sponsored by the Duponts (munitions) starting next week.'

"*My girl friend and I were at a party in the village. Someone turned on the radio. It was just when the Martians were spraying the people at Grovers Mill with the heat ray. At first we couldn't believe it was happening but it was so real we stayed glued to the radio getting more scared every minute. My girl began to cry. She wanted to be with her family. The party broke up in a hurry, our friends scattering in all directions. I drove like crazy up Sixth Avenue. I don't know how fast — fifty, maybe sixty miles an hour. The traffic cops at the street crossings just stared at us, they couldn't believe their eyes, whizzing right past them going through the red lights. I didn't care if I got a ticket. It was all over anyway. Funny thing, none of the cops chased us. I guess they were too flabbergasted. My apartment was on the way so I stopped just long enough to rush in and shout up to my father that the Martians had landed and we were all going to be killed and I was taking my girl home. When we got to her place, her parents were waiting for us. My father had called them. Told them to hold me there until he could send a doctor as I'd gone out of my mind.*"

Professor Hadley Cantril of Princeton and his research staff did an exhaustive study into the causes of the panic reactions which was published by the Princeton University Press under the title, *Invasion from Mars*. They estimated that approximately 6,000,000 listened to the program and, of that number, at least 1,200,000 took the broadcast literally and reacted according to their natures and circumstances. In addition an unknown number who were not tuned in to the broadcast were caught up in the mass hysteria.

Why were so many Americans ready to believe such a fantastic tale and why did they behave in such an irrational manner? A mere switch of the radio dial to another station broadcasting in a normal manner would have dispelled the illusion of a world catastrophe. Some listeners did switch over but a surprising number of people failed to make this simple check.

"Being in a troublesome world, anything is liable to happen. We hear so much news every day. So many things we hear are unbelievable. Like all of a sudden six hundred children burned to death in a school fire. Or a lot of people thrown out of work. Everything seems to be a shock to me."

A troublesome world. Those words, spoken by one of the women interviewed, say a great deal. High on the list of causes for the panic cited by the Princeton study is insecurity. Insecurity of all kinds — personal, economic and political. Life is insecure at best. We are here briefly, surrounded by the mysteries of our origin and significance (if any), with a tenuous hold on our environment — hostages to the fates both outside and within ourselves. Beside the uncertainties inherent in the hu-

The Sun Dial

By H. I. PHILLIPS.

Radio Broadcast, 1938.

Folks, we now take you to the Sizzling Platter Room of the Waldorf-Ansonia, where you will hear the music of Chico von Rosenbloom's orchestra.

(Number: "Pocketful of Screams.")

Announcer: Now, ladies and gentlemen, I interrupt our program to bring you a special bulletin from All-Continental Radio News. Kindly hang on to your hats.

Bulletin: Ladies and gentlemen, a comet of unusual size and ferocity has been reported by a taxicab driver in Central Park. It is approaching the earth at great speed and should be here any moment. Don't be alarmed, but look for the nearest exit.

Announcer: We return you to the music of . . . Just a minute—there seems to be another bulletin.

Bulletin: Folks, the comet has now been reported by hundreds of people and it is worse than the advance notices. It is throwing off clusters of smaller comets. The heat is terrific. A Princeton professor reports several holes burned in his coat, library and seismograph.

Announcer: I now give you the Secretary of War.

Voice: This is the Secretary of War. Hello, popper! Hello, mommer.

Announcer: O. K., Secretary.

Voice: I have called out the Army and Navy to fight the rash of comets now attacking the U. S. It is too late to save New York. Everything on Broadway has been destroyed except Lee Shubert's Mercedes car. It is indestructible. Not even a comet can get that out of Shubert Alley.

Announcer: Mr. Secretary, how

LITERAL LYMAN *NEWS ITEM:—"Thousands of listeners all over the country th the Worlds.' Believe broadcast of 'devastation' is fact."*

would you say the situation stands now?

Voice: Comets, 40; Army, 0. End of the first period.

* * *

Announcer: What about Navy?

Voice: The entire Navy first team has been destroyed by violet rays and a couple of Martians. We are putting in the second team.

Announcer: We return you to the music of Von Rosenbloom's orchestra.

* * *

Announcer: I now take you to the Consternation Room at the White House, where President Roosevelt will address you on this frightful situation which has come upon us at a time when all we expected was a half-hour of light music.

The President: My friends and neighbors, this certainly is a terrible night for comets. I have my doubts that they are comets, and

suspect they are tories. In fact, it may be a Republican plot. As the center of the disturbance seems to be in New York, I give you Governor Lehman. Governor, what is the situation at this minute? Have you been destroyed by the comets?

Governor Lehman: Those are no comets; it's just those Dewey broadcasts.

* * *

Announcer: I return you now to the music of . . .

(There is an explosion. Screams fill the air.)

* * *

Voice: What's happened?

Radio News: The main comet is in the Hudson vehicular tube, and is stalled behind a bull-fiddle and its hysterical owner, in full flight.

Voice: I give you the President of the United States, folks. Mr. President, do you concede the loss of America?

President: No; comet or no comet, I will hold the South and West.

Announcer: Ladies and gentlemen, the Secretary of Labor.

Miss Perkins: It may be Green or it may be Lewis. I am investigating.

Announcer: I give you the Secretary of Commerce.

Mr. Roper: All I can say is that we will get through this disturbance okay if business will co-operate.

Announcer: You will now hear from Secretary Ickes and Harry Hopkins.

Ickes: It's a Hoover trick.

Hopkins: As bad as this is I could stop it if I had another billion dollars.

* * *

A Policeman: Say, what's going on here, anyhow?

Announcer: We are just trying to get the radio audience away from Charlie McCarthy.

hysteria by radio play, 'War of

"At this point, we interrupt the performance to inform the radio audience that the script of our play now calls for a revolver shot. We wish to assure all who may be listening in that the shot will be fired by our sound man, using an ordinary prop revolver and <u>blank</u> cartridges. There is no cause for alarm."

"Aw, we wouldn't go down there on a bet!"

man condition are those we needlessly inflict on each other. In our highly productive but haphazard economic system we are able to produce all that we need. Yet the wealth it creates is so unevenly distributed and so much siphoned into wasteful channels that poverty, actual or marginal, is a permanent state for a large part of the world's population. In our so-called affluent society even this lopsided prosperity is anything but stable. Either we are just emerging from a depression or being admonished by bankers and politicians that one is approaching. (Only the next one won't be so bad, these oracles assure us, just a "healthy adjustment.") One wonders whose health they have in mind.

Many responses of those interviewed showed a definite connection between their economic insecurity and their susceptibility to panic as in the following three cases:

"Ever since my husband lost his job a few years ago, things seem to have gone from bad to worse. I don't know when everything will be all right again."

"As you see, I'm a colored man. My color is against me wherever I turn. I can't get as good a job as I think I deserve and no matter how hard I try certain positions are closed to me and I have to live, work and play where the white folks dictate."

"I haven't been employed for four years on ac-

*count of the depression and I don't know how long
my brother's job will last."*

In 1938, the year of the broadcast, the deep depression of the early thirties was still vivid in the
memories of all adults. They had experienced the
shock of losing their jobs or their businesses or
their farms overnight. Many saw their families
hungry and some homeless as the banks foreclosed
mortgages on a vast scale. The solid rock of our
social structure turned out to be quicksand.

*"The announcer said a meteor had fallen from
Mars and I was sure he thought that but in the
back of my head I had an idea that the meteor was
just a camouflage. It was really an airplane like a
zeppelin that looked like a meteor and the Germans were attacking us with gas bombs."*

Add to all the other anxieties the shadow of war
creeping toward us during the thirties. As we
know, war is not a spontaneous phenomenon, it
is only the intensification of forces already at work
during the interludes of peace like humidity gather-
ing before a storm. When the fighting actually
starts, it often comes as a relief since we have
already endured the suspense. The Martians were
on the move long before the night of the symbolic
invasion. Many listeners translated the monstrous
creatures into Germans. They assumed that Hitler

had developed a secret devastating weapon and was taking over the whole world. In one terror-filled night our accumulated fears and insecurities came home to roost.

"When those things landed, I thought the best thing to do was to go away, so I took $3.25 out of my savings and bought a ticket. After I'd gone sixty miles, I heard it was a play. Now I don't have any money left for the shoes I was saving up for. Would you please have someone send me a pair of black shoes, size 9 B."

This pathetic letter addressed to Orson from an uneducated laborer illustrates another factor in one's susceptibility to a panic reaction. Although college graduates were not immune, the Cantril study showed that the response to the broadcast varied in proportion to the amount of education. In general, those with more schooling had acquired a more reliable critical standard which enabled them to assess the credibility of the events in the radio play against their knowledge of the world. An invasion from another planet was too fantastic to believe, it didn't accord with their conception of reality. Besides too many things happened in too short a time. Also to many educated listeners the voice of Orson Welles was a familiar one. They knew Orson as a man of many attainments but not the astronomer he portrayed as Professor Pierson in the broadcast.

In some cases coincidence added fuel to the imaginary fires that were spreading over cities and countrysides. In the small town of Concrete, Washington, there was a local power failure at the very moment when the Martians in the play were supposedly disrupting the nation's communication and power sources. To the local listeners, suddenly plunged into darkness as the lights went out all over town, it seemed a confirmation of what they believed was happening all over the country. The result was mass hysteria, families fleeing wildly in the night, isolated from any information source that might allay their terror.

Miss Jane Dean, an unmarried woman, fifty-seven years old, with a strong Protestant religious background, took an entirely different view of the invading Martians as she later recalled:

"I knew the forces of God were overwhelming us and we were being given punishment at last for our evil ways."

In her case the approaching holocaust was a vindication of her beliefs and an opportunity to expiate her guilts. When she found out later that the broadcast was only a play, her first reaction was anger — she felt cheated. She had done all that praying for nothing. On second thought she said she was glad she'd asked for forgiveness even if she didn't have to. It was like money stored up in a heavenly bank.

Her reaction may seem somewhat extreme but religious fundamentalism is still a potent influence on the thinking and behavior of many Americans, especially in the South where, incidentally, the panic reaction was relatively more severe than in other geographical areas. Members of various sects gather every so often to await the apocalyptic day when the world will come to an end. Fortunately for most of us but no doubt disappointing to them, our little planet has so far managed to survive their predictions. To such believers, unwilling to face the realities of the world, the Martians appeared not as monsters but as destroying angels sent to redeem sinful humanity and open the gates of heaven.

"Dad kept calling, 'O God, do what you can to save us. . . .'"

The average twentieth century man is not a fanatic. The Gershwin lyrics in *Porgy and Bess,* "I takes the gospel wherever it's poss'ble," may reflect the unconscious attitude of most people today who call themselves Christians. The demonstrable findings of science have eroded our faith in the unprovable assumptions of organized religion. The man quoted above, even in his extremity, is not certain that God can save him. The most he can pray for is "Do what you can . . ." All of us would like to believe in an All-Powerful Being watching over us and taking care of us. But too many contradicions stare us in the face every time we hear the news on television or read the papers. If there is such a Being, this world of ours, bloodstained and tragedy-ridden, must either have escaped His notice or been given up as a bad job.

I have a vivid recollection of a televised scene during the severe hurricane of 1969 which devastated sections of the South. In a small Mississippi town a number of stunned and bedraggled survivors, many of whose homes were destroyed, were gathered in a church service. The preacher was attempting to reconcile the disaster with Christian doctrine. The storm, he contended, was a demonstration and warning of God's power and, at the same time, a proof of his mercy that so many, including those present, had been spared. To anyone observing the scene, the unanswerable question came to mind: "But what about those three hundred persons who were not spared?"

"My knees were shaking so I could hardly climb the stairs. I found my nephew had come back home and gone to bed. I woke him up. I looked in the icebox and saw some chicken left over from Sunday dinner I was saving for Monday night dinner. I said to my nephew, 'We may as well eat this chicken — we won't be here in the morning.'"

Often at a moment of extremity some trivial act will occur to us as it did to this woman who thought of her uneaten chicken in somewhat the way a prisoner in the death cell might regard his last meal before his execution. A final attempt at making life seem to go on as usual.

When I was fourteen, my grandfather died and I was taken to the funeral by my parents. It was my first contact with death in a personal sense. My grandfather was a Grand Army veteran of the Civil War and the graveside service was attended by the surviving members of his post along with family, relatives and friends. The scene is still vivid in my memory. Muffled drums played taps — I thought they would never stop. Hysterical shrieks and weeping followed the coffin into the grave. Right afterward I followed the grown-ups to the cemetery restaurant where a dinner was served. Now the mood had changed completely. Relatives who had been beside themselves with grief a few minutes ago were chatting with each other while they attacked the meal with famished appetites. In spite of parental urging, I couldn't eat. I just sat and watched and wondered. How could they forget so quickly? . . . Of course they hadn't forgotten. I realize that now many years later. Whether leaving death behind or facing it in the form of Martian invaders, eating is a natural affirmation of life's continuity.

"The broadcast had us all worried but I knew it would at least scare ten years life out of my mother-in-law."

Some listeners, like this man, had ambivalent feelings about the approaching holocaust. He didn't like the destruction the Martians were wreaking but, if the invasion got his mother-in-law off his back a little sooner, at least there was a silver lining.

"My only thought was delight that if the Martians came to Stelton, I wouldn't have to pay the butcher's bill."

Evidently this man was so weighed down with debts that he would rather take his chances with the Martians than with his creditors, reminding us of the truth of Thoreau's words — that a great many of us live our lives in quiet desperation.

"I was looking forward with some pleasure to the destruction of the human race. If we're to have Fascist domination of the world, there is no purpose in living anyway."

Apparently this listener, interviewed by the Princeton research team, was so convinced that fascism would spread over the earth, he preferred a quick end at the hands of the Martians.

"I was thrilled. It was the most exciting thing ever happened to me. I ran all through my apart-

ment building telling everybody the Martians were here."

To this woman anything was preferable to a dull existence, even a catastrophe. And there is a tendency to enjoy spreading bad news. It takes some of the sting out of it and lends a sense of personal importance. Since this news could hardly be worse, she was apparently intoxicated with her role as the apartment-house Cassandra — until the truth deflated her euphoria.

"Dan, why don't you get dressed? You don't want to die in your working-clothes."

The proprieties must be observed, as this woman reminded her husband. For such an important occasion as death, one should be properly attired, preferably in a dark suit, a white shirt and necktie. Many of us live and die in the straightjacket of the prevailing fashions and mores. No wonder the youth of today are offending their elders. Shaggy hair, unkempt dungarees, Indian beads . . . Certainly no way to meet a visiting Martian.

"I believed the broadcast as soon as I heard the professor from Princeton and the officials in Washington. I knew it was an awfully dangerous situation when all those military men were there and the Secretary of State spoke."

Status. Unfortunately, we are ready to believe almost anything if it comes from a recognized authority. This man gave complete credibility to the "news bulletins" from the nonexistent Intercontinental Radio News because important men were supposedly making the announcements. He mentioned the "Secretary of State" although it was actually the fictional Secretary of the Interior whose Rooseveltian voice came over the air. Instead of hearing what was actually said, the listener heard what accorded with his preconceptions. However, it is interesting to note that while people believed the "information" government officials were giving out about the gravity of the situation, they were not ready to take their advice to put their trust in the military forces of this nation. It seems that was the moment many listeners chose to reach for their hats and depart for distant places.

The social and psychological factors which contributed to the panic were not confined to America. A year or so after our program a radio production group in Lima, Peru, appropriated the play, translated it into Spanish and broadcast it to their countrymen. Again a panic occurred but on a smaller scale since there were fewer radios within the broadcast range. However, the aftermath was even more drastic — in keeping, perhaps, with the Latin temperament. When the Peruvians found out they had been tricked and the world wasn't coming to an end, they decided to put an end, at least, to the offending radio station, burning it to the ground. Since then, we have tried to keep the Martian genii in a bottle tightly corked with a warning label "open at your peril."

IV

A MARTIAN VISITS THE
SCENE OF HIS CRIME

". . . wild night."

Grovers Mill, New Jersey, a hamlet of two hundred souls, more or less, six miles from Princeton, with not even a post office it can call its own, boasts two distinctions which keep it resolutely on the tourist maps. Through its farmland flows one of four streams on the North American mainland which run, perversely, north instead of south; and here, on its placid acres, the first Martian landed and used his devastating heat ray on human targets.

Since it was Hallowe'en — the thirtieth plus one anniversary of the bizarre event — I decided it was an appropriate time to visit Grovers Mill and find out what memories of the "invasion" had survived the years. Enough time had elapsed, I assumed, that I could safely confess my contribution to whatever distress the broadcast had caused its inhabitants. As usual, my tape recorder wasn't working but my wife volunteered to go along. Anne has many of the attributes of a recorder including almost total recall and a full complement of sound effects which she can reproduce at the slightest provocation. I knew I could count on her not only to play back the voices of those we interviewed but even the sounds of whatever farm animals, birds or insects might be lurking in the background.

Grovers Mill is so small you can drive right through it without knowing you were there — which is exactly what we did. Backtracking, we stopped at the old mill for which the hamlet was named. Across from it was a feedstore which sold produce to the farmers in the area. No other stores, no lunchroom, not even a gas station. How could we strike up a conversation when the whole place seemed deserted?

Then came our first break. A middle-aged, clean-shaven man emerged from the feedstore. Since his hair was graying, I figured he must have been alive at the time of the broadcast. I shall call him Mr. Garrison although that is not his real name. When we introduced ourselves, he was friendly but he looked a little harassed as though he had things on his mind more pressing than Martians. When we told him the purpose of our visit was to research what happened in Grovers Mill on that famous, or infamous, October night, he gave a wan smile which said as plainly as words, "Oh, no, not that again."

After he told us how often he had been inter-

*Wilson farm, Grovers Mill. Where the
first Martians landed.*

The mill.

viewed over the intervening years by newsmen, radio commentators, feature article writers and social scientists, we could appreciate that the subject of Martians had lost some of its bloom. However, when I mentioned that I had written the radio play which the Mercury Theatre had broadcast, he became more interested. It turned out that he was the grandson of the Mr. Wilson on whose farm the first Martian was supposed to have landed. Actually, the name of the farmer I had used in the script was Wilmuth but the reporters covering the story had conveniently changed it to Wilson so that they had a definite site to photograph.

From Mr. Garrison we learned that the mill across the road, which is still in operation, is over two hundred years old. He pointed to the doorway where the then owner of the mill had taken his stand, shotgun in hand, ready to repel those "foreigners" if they showed their cowled heads. This scene was replayed the next day for the benefit of the news photographers and was the one so widely pictured in the metropolitan papers. Before Mr. Garrison left us to attend to his business, he suggested we drive to Cranbury, five miles away, remarking that there was "considerable excitement there on that night."

Cranbury is an attractive, pre-Revolutionary War town which serves as the post office and business center for the surrounding farm communities in-

cluding Grovers Mill. Our first stop was at a gas
station on the main street. It was a lucky chance.
Spotting us as strangers, a passerby strolled up to
us remarking on the weather which we agreed was
October at its best. The man, whom I shall call Mr.
Mathews, looked like a woodsman, his flesh droop-
ing, hound-dog fashion, as though it had outgrown
his massive frame. Two gold teeth shone like headlights from his grizzled but amiable face. He liked
to talk and he'd found a willing audience. At the
time of the broadcast Mr. Mathews was the fire
chief of the town, a "temporary" job which lasted
fifteen years. As he recalled the events of that Hallowe'en night, he shook his head in disbelief. Calls
kept coming in reporting fires in the woods set off
by the Martian heat rays. As a result he spent most
of the night chasing fires that were never lit. In
the course of covering the countryside in answer
to these false alarms, he had an opportunity to
witness what was going on in the area — in his
words "a wild night." Farmers, armed with guns,
roamed the countryside looking for Martians or
for the militia which was supposedly being deployed against the "enemy" at Grovers Mill. Later
over a hundred New Jersey state troopers were dispatched to the area to calm the populace and dis-
arm these volunteer defenders "before somebody
got hurt."

Mr. Mathews chuckled as he recalled some of
the more humorous incidents. One distraught lo-

Ready to repel those foreigners. (William Dock, at that time, age 76.)

cal resident, anxious to reach his wife's family in Pennsylvania before the world ended, jumped in his car without taking the time to open the garage door. When his wife screamed a warning, he paid no attention, gunning the motor and driving right through the door with a splintering crash, yelling back at his wife, "We won't be needing it anymore."

The rest of the story may be true or it may be the work of Mr. Mathews's imagination stimulated by our avid interest. When a day later the couple returned to their home with the world still intact but with their garage partly demolished, the husband was so furious at the deception he again gunned the motor on entering the garage. His foot slipped off the brake and the car, out of control, smashed right through the rear wall. With the help of the Martians he had converted his garage into an instant carport.

Another neighbor, a real estate broker, had been listening to the broadcast as he emptied a bottle of whiskey. It proved a potent combination. His chow dog, undisturbed by the invading Martians, was sleeping peacefully at his feet. For some reason he thought the dog would be safer from the approaching monsters in a wired-off kennel on one side of the house. He grabbed the dog and, rushing out of doors, tried to toss the animal over the fence into the kennel. The chow, bewildered and frightened by his master's strange behavior, locked his jaw on his sleeve. In his effort to break the hold, the man swung the dog over his head several times, the chow hanging on until the sleeve ripped off.

Finally freed from the beast, the man sped off in his car to his brother's house, yanked the dozing man from his chair and into the car. The brother, who knew nothing of the broadcast, was as bewildered as the chow dog. Between the Martians and the liquor, the realtor was in no condition to explain. His passenger, holding on to the seat for dear life as the car raced madly up one road and down another, kept trying to find out what it was all about but he got no coherent answer. All the time the car radio was running but he was in such fear for his brother's sanity and his own life, he hadn't paid any attention. However, the soothing words of a radio commentator finally penetrated, with the reassurance that the Martians that had panicked a nation were merely characters in a play. What the kidnapped man said to his inebriated brother at this point is not recorded.

Thanking Mr. Mathews, we drove to the Cranbury Inn, a rambling Colonial tavern founded, according to the sign outside, in 1780. After lunch I wandered into the taproom hoping to pick up more information. A slight, gray-haired man sat alone at one end of the bar staring into his martini glass. I took a stool beside him and struck up a conversation. When he found out what I was after, he became determinedly coy, "I could tell you some things about that night would make your hair stand on end."

My hair was ready, in fact anxious to stand on end, so I asked him, "What things?" Immediately he backed away from the subject and began to tell me all he knew about Orson Welles which wasn't very much, mostly what he'd read of Orson's life in Spain and his intense interest in bullfighting — which may or may not be true.

Concealing my impatience, I tried tactfully to bring the subject back to the Martians. But he parried by asking me where I came from. When I told him Woodstock, New York, this launched him on a long tirade about the Woodstock Festival and "all those damn hippies." To prove he was an authority on the subject, he informed me he used to be a justice of the peace. By this time I began to feel I was on trial for living in a town that harbored hippies and that I had personally launched the Woodstock Festival. My real crime which I had confessed to — helping to launch a Martian attack on his community — didn't concern him. Realizing that I never would learn about "those things that would make my hair stand on end" I withdrew as gracefully as possible. His last remark, said with a sly grin, followed me out: "Well, I'll bet that set you back a yard or two." When I rejoined Anne at the car, I told her my frustrating "interview." She was philosophical. "Well, let's make up the lost yardage."

"I don't see nothing." (*Mr. and Mrs. William Anderson of the Wilson farm.*)

A chance remark of Mr. Mathews that some shots had actually been fired at a supposed Martian took us to a prosperous-looking farmhouse adjacent to the mill. Behind the house was the object that had been mistaken for one of the "invaders." It was a tall, topless windmill with spidery metal legs supporting a rounded block of reddish-colored wood (the Martian face?) which was the base of the missing windmill blades. Possibly the story of bullets shattering the structure is apocryphal but we were struck with its resemblance to a Martian machine as pictured in various illustrations.

Our next stop was at the Wilson farm, consisting of a house, barn and a number of outbuildings, all looking somewhat seared and desolate as though the heat ray had raked them. On the surrounding acres a dozen or so Herefords were grazing. The present tenants were a Scandinavian couple who had worked for the original Mr. Wilson and were there on the night of the invasion. And the word "invasion" is used here in a literal sense. The invaders, however, were not Martians but sightseers. Hundreds of cars poured into the farmyard that night, the next day and for weeks afterward.

The couple, whom I shall call the Jensens, were not exactly delighted to see us, which was understandable in view of the long harassment they had undergone as a result of the broadcast. Mrs. Jensen took a formidable stance in front of the kitchen door as though to bar entrance. Mr. Jensen, who looked like a somewhat damaged Peter Sellers, was halfway up a stepladder and remained there. Our brief interview was made more difficult by a language gap, their English being only slightly better than our Scandinavian. When I inquired whether they had made money charging tourists for the privilege of "seeing the spot where the Martians landed" as reported in some news columns, there was a chorus of indignant denials. Mr. Jensen mumbled a long speech, roughly translated as: "That Orson Welles. His father lives up the road. How would he like it if a thousand cars parked on his land and trampled his crops . . ." One sentence made us prick up our ears. Orson's father living in Grovers Mill! Where? But that was all to be gotten from the Jensens except a vague gesture in the direction of the mill.

Back to the mill. Yes, there is an elderly man by that name — second house on the right after the crossroads. Excited by the possibility of a small miracle, we drove to the house but the name on the mailbox was "Wells" and not "Welles" as Orson spells it. I decided to chance it anyway. The venerable gentleman who answered the doorbell shook his head but pointed up the road. He was no relation but Orson himself had lived in the guesthouse of the Cotswald cottage at the top of the hill. Unbelievable! I had selected Grovers Mill in the play by closing my eyes and jabbing the pencil into a New Jersey road map. The mathematical odds that Orson had lived in this out-of-the-way hamlet must have been at least a thousand to one.

. . . mistaken for one of the invaders.

Yet it was true. Mrs. Carl Sjorstrom, a warm and hospitable woman, was entertaining some guests in her garden and she quickly included us in the company. When we told her the purpose of our visit, she beamed. Yes, Orson Welles, as a very young man, spent a summer in the small guest apartment writing a book. She showed us into the one-room annex which was only large enough for the full-sized bed and a writing table. However, the window looked out on a charming garden with a path leading down to a pond. Still finding it difficult to believe the coincidence, we tried to imagine Orson living in this rather austere room in contrast to the elegance of his later life. It wasn't exactly from log cabin to the White House but it had a certain Alger story-book quality. Mrs. Sjorstrom generously invited us to spend the night there but, while we admire Orson, we had no particular desire to sleep in his bed. And we had one more lead to follow up, this time in Princeton seven miles away.

Each Hallowe'en evening station WHWH in Princeton rebroadcasts parts of the radio play along with accounts of what happened throughout the area the night of its original broadcast. Since the producer of the program must have done considerable research over the years, we made an appointment to meet him at the studio.

It was evening when we drove down Nassau Street, glowing with lights from the mullioned windows of the university. It was our first sight of the campus with its gray Gothic towers and spacious lawns. As we watched the students strolling in and out of the quadrangles, I hoped that no Martian of our own species would ever disturb its tranquility as our imaginary ones had done on that far-off October night. We passed the observatory where our fictional Professor Pierson had first spied that "orange flash of light on the planet Mars." This reminded us of the actual Princeton professors who had been told that "something of an unusual nature, possibly a meteorite, had landed in Grovers Mill." The two men spent most of a frustrating night looking for the object without being aware they were stalking a Martian. At the radio station we were told that the two professors had to endure a lot of ribbing from their colleagues, "Found any hot meteorites lately?"

Ed Klein, a lanky, loose-hinged, good-natured man in his thirties, was the producer in charge of the annual program on the Martian broadcast. Although he was "on the air," he entertained us in one of the studios, recounting stories while doing the seemingly impossible task of feeding two record players, making spot announcements every minute on the minute, selecting tapes of weather forecasts, traffic conditions and political advertisements, clicking them into playbacks at appropriate moments, all done very casually, the only sign of strain being some badly bitten fingernails.

Some of the incidents he had researched were by now familiar ones but others had some unique

. . . *and the villagers still talk about it.*

aspects, proving that the possibilities of human behavior in a panic situation are practically infinite.
Up to now we had never heard of anyone who
started off knowing it was a play but was so caught
up in it that what began as fantasy became reality
in the mind of the listener. Mrs. K. was an intelligent woman who listened regularly to the Mercury
Theatre programs and was looking forward to the
advertised *The War of the Worlds*. On her way
home from a meeting she turned on the car radio
to the CBS station where the play was being broadcast. By the time the Martians were wading the
Hudson River to occupy New York City, she was
driving through red lights in a frantic effort to
reach her family before it was too late. She burst
into the house screaming for them to take shelter
in the cellar. Slowly she sputtered to a stop as her
husband sat there looking up at her with a quiz-
zical smile. The Philharmonic was playing sooth-
ingly over the radio on another station.

The night produced heroes as well as victims.
Besides the farmers who were prepared to face the
Martians with shotguns, there was a man living
in the neighboring city of New Brunswick who
was fleeing from the "invaders" as they advanced
on his area. He had driven ten miles when he remembered that his dog was tied up in the backyard
of his home. Unwilling to let the animal starve, he
was courageous enough to drive back to rescue his
pet even though the cowled head of a Martian
might appear in his path at any moment.

In a neighborhood church the minister was preaching a sermon in the Sunday evening service. Suddenly a wild-eyed man rushed into the church with the news that the Martians were invading the country, several of them as close as the Pulaski Skyway. The congregation were put to a stern test. Should they break and run or stay where they were, relying on God's protection? After all, they were in His house. With great self-control the minister went on with his sermon. Not a person left. However, when the service was over, there was a mass rush for the doors. No one stayed to shake hands with the minister.

The next morning we left Princeton with a warm feeling toward people in general and a negative feeling toward Martians, real or imaginary, domestic or interplanetary. As for Grovers Mill itself, we shall remember it as perhaps the only historical site in the world where the event that made it memorable never happened.

MARS: FACT AND LEGEND

"A planet of ebbing life . . ."

When H. G. Wells chose Mars as the planet which launched the invasion against the earth, it was no random selection. In the early mythology of Greece and Rome, Mars (Ares in Greek) was the warrior god of strife and slaughter. Under favorable conditions the planet which bore his name is easily distinguished from the others by its reddish tinge. No doubt the ancients associated its color with the shedding of blood, which would account for its bellicose reputation.

The god Mars, of course, was the son of Jupiter and Juno and it seems that his parents, while not exactly approving of him, rather enjoyed some of his more spectacular antics. On the other hand his sister Minerva was not amused, particularly when he harassed the Greeks whom she favored in the Trojan War. In spite of his ferocious nature, Mars was constantly bested by his more intelligent sister. On one occasion when he misbehaved, she seized his lance and thrust it through his middle.

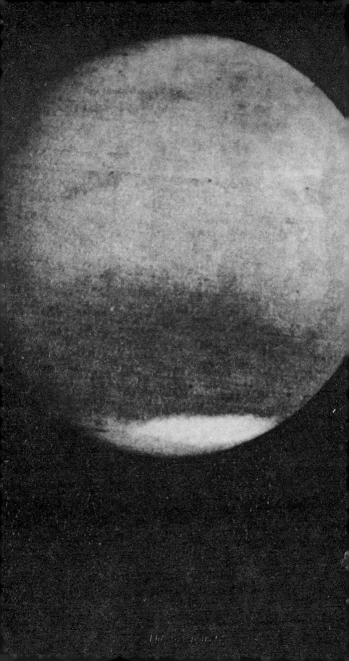
The real planet

Naturally he was indignant at this unsisterly act and complained to his father. However, there was not even a rumble from Olympus; it was Jupiter's policy not to interfere in family tiffs. Mars being an immortal, his pierced flesh soon healed and he was ready for more mischief.

His private life was equally incontinent. When he wasn't occupied fighting, he was seducing mortal women even though his Olympian mistress was no less a catch than Venus, the goddess of love. This mating of sex and violence produced four sons — Terror, Trembling, Fear and the last was named, as it turned out prophetically, Panic.

In early Rome the third month marked the beginning of military campaigns and was named, appropriately, March. It was ushered in by a festival with priests carrying sacred shields and lances as they danced through the city streets singing the praises of Mars. When the campaigns ended in October, a horse was sacrificed to the god, his head and bloody tail cut off and laid on the altar of Vesta and attended by the Vestal Virgins.

Many campaigns of Caesar and other Roman generals were waged against their fierce tribal neighbors to the north, the Germans, whose god, Ziu, was identified with Mars. The emblem he adopted from ancient sources was the swastika. The symbols of folk legend are long-lived; they have a way of reappearing in the recurring cycles of history.

The planet Mars emerged from the realm of

myth to come under the observation of science from the time Galileo first viewed it through his primitive telescope. Since then it has become the most controversial of all planets. The astronomers after Galileo developed various conflicting theories depending on their interpretation of certain features unique to the planet. As the range and power of telescopes increased and these features came into clearer view, one theory would displace another. Naturally much of the speculation centered on whether or not there was life on Mars and, if so, what kind of life.

In 1877 the Italian astronomer Schiaparelli recorded a large number of what he termed *canali* on the surface of the planet. These canal-like crevices were confirmed by others, notably the American astronomer Percival Lowell, who established the famous observatory at Flagstaff, Arizona. For a time these canals or crevices stirred great excitement in scientific circles since they suggested the possibility of intelligent life on our neighboring planet. Since then, these indentations on the Martian landscape have been found to be less straight and artificial-looking than was supposed by Schiaparelli and Lowell and the recent pictures sent back by Mariner 6 have all but foreclosed the possibility of Martian-made canals.

However, in 1960 the Soviet scientist Shklovsky came out with an ingenious theory. Conceding that there is no evidence of advanced forms of life on the surface of the planet today, he suggested it was possible that intelligent beings once existed there before atmospheric conditions became too hostile. From observing their behavior, he concluded that the two moons, Phobus and Deimos, which orbit around Mars are not composed of solid rock but are hollow and, therefore, are not natural satellites at all but artificial space stations built by a departed race.

A corollary to this hypothesis was advanced by another Soviet scientist, Davidov, that such an intelligent race, if it ever existed, adapted to a changing atmosphere on the surface of the planet by "going underground" to find conditions necessary to their survival. This fanciful notion is predicated on the view that Mars, in the words of an earlier astronomer, is "a planet of ebbing life," having once possessed oxygen-rich atmosphere which leaked away. Since there are no observable lakes or oceans on Mars at the present time, this theory assumes that the surface water froze and was then overlaid with dust. The polar caps, with their thin icy or frosty coating, give some credence to this conjecture.

While these theories are not widely accepted, they can't be entirely ruled out until we can examine the planet's crust to see whether it contains fossils. Since both the United States and the Soviet Union project landings on Mars, either by manned or unmanned flights, the question may finally be resolved before the end of the century.

Until then the weight of scientific evidence sup-

Mariner VII photo showing a trace of water frost or dry
ice around the polar caps.

ports the view that, whatever its past, Mars today is unsuitable for intelligent beings or even advanced plant forms. However, recent studies by Dr. Robert Sharp of the California Institute of Technology and Dr. George Pinmenter of the University of California, based on the photographs sent back by Mariners 6 and 7, tend to support the view that Mars is not a dead planet like the moon. There is at least a strong probability that some form of organic life exists there, possibly in the damp region near the south polar ice cap. If such organisms exist, they could either be similar to some found on earth or entirely alien, as difficult for us to imagine as a new color outside our familiar spectrum.

Among other unique features, these photographs reveal a chaotic terrain of jumbled hills and valleys extending over several hundred thousand miles, unlike anything seen on the moon or even on earth on such a vast scale. Moreover, this region, brighter than the surrounding terrain, should be cooler than the dark areas which absorb more solar heat. Instead, the studies show that it is two degrees warmer. Another mystery is why some regions on the planet become darker in spring, once attributed to the growth of vegetation and now a question mark which can only be answered by exploratory flights closer to its surface.

Whatever relations we humans develop with our neighbor in the solar system, let us fervently hope that we'll act with neighborly restraint. By mindless waste and exploitation of our natural resources we have damaged our own planet to such an extent that, unless a drastic reversal occurs within the next decade, the earth may also become "a planet of ebbing life." Another danger exists. Organisms on Mars may be contagious to us or we to them. For our mutual protection extreme caution will have to be exercised in any contact between the planets. And it would be a hopeful sign for the future if the two super-powers would cooperate in this great venture instead of letting it degenerate into another race to put this or that flag on the Martian landscape.

Not long ago there was a chilling prediction by an official in the American State Department. He projected a plan, which apparently his science advisors considered feasible, for launching a spaceship armed with nuclear missiles that could push the moon Phobus out of the Mars gravitational field across space and into our orbit. This little satellite, only twelve miles in diameter, would make a convenient, ready-made space station for whatever purpose, military or civilian, we chose to use it.

Apart from its questionable use, the hazards inherent in such a project are obvious. There would be many unknown factors to deal with and a slight miscalculation could send the kidnapped moon crashing down on earth. Now belatedly we are learning the dangers of upsetting the ecological balance of our own world. Science tells us that there is an analogous balance of interdependent forces in the solar system. We disturb that balance at our peril. In our society larceny is considered a crime unless practiced on a large enough scale like robbing a weaker country of its natural resources. A celestial theft of such a magnitude as snatching Phobus from its parent planet could turn out to be our final felony.

Once man believed he stood at the center of the universe and all the heavenly bodies revolved around him. Many of his religious ideas stemmed from this egocentric view. When Galileo asserted that the earth was merely one of the planets circling the sun, as we know, he was persecuted by the church. Modern telescopes like Palomar have opened up new conceptions of the universe. Now we know that our solar system is not even central to our own galaxy; it is tucked off in a far corner. So vast is this spiral nebula which we call the Milky Way that a beam of light, traveling at the speed of 186,000 miles a second, takes a hundred thousand years to cross from one end to the other. And outside our immediate galaxy billions of star systems extend beyond the reach of even our most powerful telescopes into the mists of scientific conjecture.

By all the mathematical laws of probability, in this vast aggregate of galaxies there must exist numberless planets with environmental conditions similar to our own and capable of developing intelligent life. Possibly some have evolved far be-

yond man's present state "with minds that are to
our minds as ours are to the beasts in the jungle."
While life such as ours is unlikely to be found in
the solar system, it is almost a certainty that in the
universe at large we are not alone.

For several years my wife and I lived on the
desert. Evenings we would sit out in the patio and
watch night come down. But "come down" is not
an accurate description. The roof seemed to lift off
our little planet, revealing not just a sky above us
but the whole universe wrapped around us. The
stars hung as globes from the blackness of inter-
stellar space, so close they could be touched by the
naked eye. Astronomy was made visible.

It was surely not a cozy universe that was un-
veiled and some of our guests were disturbed by its
immensity made so manifest. "Doesn't it make you
feel small and insignificant? . . ." No, not if you
feel a part of it, if you share in its wonder and
mystery. For human eyes can track the stars over
millions of light years and man-made instruments
are able to range much further and human intelligence can speculate on what is beyond reach of
our senses or our instruments. Even if the universe
is infinite, so it seems is the mind of man. The
thing conceived and that which conceives it are
two aspects of a single reality.

In the physical world the speed of light is
considered an ultimate; yet how much faster is
thought. It takes eight minutes for light to reach
us from the sun and four and a half years from the

nearest star. For the human mind there is no time lag. When we think of something we are already there — whether it's a point in space or an abstract concept.

Man has walked on the moon and, whatever our reservations, we can all agree it was a masterwork of technology as well as an heroic achievement. Mars is the next target in our space program and perhaps eventually we will reach the other planets in our solar system. But as far as physical travel is concerned, this seems to be the end of the road. George Wald, the eminent Harvard biologist, estimates that the nearest star with a planet capable of supporting life in any advanced form is over ten light years away. Since there seems to be no way of traveling at the speed of light without *being* light, such a journey to a destination unknown would take many lifetimes. At least in a physical sense, the stars are not for us.

The earth is our home and we would do well to cherish it. As the astronauts were flying back from the sterile wasteland of the moon, they looked upon our world, clothed in its bluish atmosphere, and found it incredibly beautiful. When we are able to view the earth not as real estate or a dump for our industrial waste or a fief to be plundered, we may not need to go out into space to appreciate its beauty and its bounty.

Yet it is the nature of man to venture. He cannot stand still. Evolution is forever prodding him to take the next step even though he may not know where the steps are leading him. He felt the urge to move faster and farther than his legs would carry him and he invented the wheel; he watched the flight of birds and he invented wings; he looked up at the stars and invented the rocket. But now that we are nearing the boundaries of geographical exploration, the question arises — what next?

In this area of conjecture one must take the risk of letting his hopes and desires influence his speculations. However that may be, I have an abiding conviction that the great adventure of humankind will not be in outer space but in inner space — that vast, untraversed region between man's present state of consciousness and his psychic potential. Except for our philosophers, our poets and mystics, we have used our minds almost solely in the service of what we considered our practical needs: survival, the aggrandizement of our egos and our material fortunes. Much of our technology has been merely the extension of our ability to wrest things from nature or from each other. Our present society sanctifies this competition under the hallowed name of individualism. Yet our experience proves over and over again that there is nothing less fulfilling to an individual life than the unrestrained and aggressive exercise of his ego. His "cup never runneth over" because, no matter how much he pours in it, his cup is bottomless and remains empty.

How often we hear the expression that by this

or that act "man has conquered space" or "man has conquered nature." You'd think the natural world was our enemy instead of the environment which nurtures us. The truth is we are as much a part of nature as the nearest tree or the farthest star. When we war on nature by misusing or exploiting it, we war on ourselves. Little wonder then that we war on each other. The Martians are not coming to take over the earth on this or any other Hallowe'en; they are already here, a greater menace to our survival than any monsters from other worlds.

The American Indian was aware of his union with nature — it was the basis of his religion — and we might have learned more from him had we not been so busy robbing him of his land and "conquering the West." It is no accident that many of our youth today rejecting our culture are wearing Indian beads and adopting a form of tribal life. As far as I can see, they have no interest in "conquering" anything. They are looking inward, seeking by meditation, music and sometimes by drugs to transcend the limitations of their senses, to "blow their minds" as they put it, meaning to expand their consciousness by direct contact with its source, the "cosmic mind" referred to in Arthur Clarke's *Childhood's End*.

Admittedly this probe into the psychic is stumbling, often irrational and sometimes dangerous, but every experiment of any dimension takes its toll. Whether or not they achieve the breakthrough they vaguely envisage, at least they are taking the first bold step into practically virgin territory which could yield more in human terms than anything we might find on other planets.

For generations past, love has been preached from every pulpit and freedom from every political platform, but many of today's youth, taking a fresh, hard look at the actions of our society, find the truth veiled behind the fine words. The age difference is nothing compared to the ethical gap which separates them from their parents' generation. Free from the need of material possessions as a status symbol to bolster their egos, they share with each other what they have — which is the essence of love.

Under conditions that would appall their elders, four hundred thousand of them came together at a music festival and became an instant community. No leader was elected, no organization was needed — it was person to person. Hands touched hands, bread was shared and the miracle of the loaves became a symbolic reality.

In the words of a young girl named Judy, who was there and later interviewed by the *New York Times:* "I just had a feeling, wow, there were so many of us, we really have power." Yes, there will be fifty million youths like Judy within the next five years according to a census estimate and, if they remain true to their own values, they *will* have power. This should be a warning to earthly

"I just had a feeling, wow, there were so many of us . . ."

Martians, those of high position and low performance. Love, multiplied by fifty million, could clean our air, our water, our cities and restore our wounded world. We may even find flowers growing out of the barrel of our guns.

VI

THE PRIVILEGED VOICE

"People can be made to swallow poison . . ."

By 1938 the radio was exercising a powerful influence on many areas of our lives as the photograph from the *New York Times* illustrates. Charlie McCarthy was making us laugh, Benny Goodman was making us dance, Toscanini and Wallenstein were giving us classical music, Prime Minister Chamberlain was selling us Munich and President Roosevelt was giving us the confidence to climb out of the worst depression in our history. Our unwitting contribution in that last year before World War II was to scare the country out of its wits — quite literally.

Radio made us aware of how different voices affect us. Orson's resonant, throbbing voice can invest a simple declarative sentence with a sense of excitement and importance. When early in the Martian broadcast, the reporter asks for an explanation of the strange eruptions on the planet Mars and Orson, as Professor Pierson, replies, "I cannot account for it," he is able to convey in those few

RADIO'S INTERNATIONAL CAVALCADE

Arturo Toscanini lengthened his radio season for 1938-39; Ignace Jan Paderewski at a piano in the Alps played his first American radio recital in 1938; Orson Welles dramatized "The War of the Worlds" so effectively that he gave American radio its first "panic."

Clockwise: Edgar Bergen and Charlie McCarthy enter 1939 at the top of the popularity polls; Benny Goodman, Pied Piper of the jitterbugs "swings" them into a New Year; Prime Minister Chamberlain broadcast 1938's most emotional and dramatic plea for peace; Max Jordan "scooped" all broadcasters at Munich by reading the Four-Power Pact seventeen minutes after it was signed.

Alfred Wallenstein, conductor, who continues his crusade for good music on the air; he added the Bach Cantatas to radio in 1938.

Professor Quiz, whose ethereal puzzle idea spread to many wave lengths in 1938.

President Roosevelt broadcast thirty-two times in 1938; two were "fireside chats."
HEADLINE PERFORMERS WHO MADE HISTORY, MUSIC AND DRAMA ON THE AIR IN 1938.

words a sense of foreboding and impending drama. Chamberlain's modulated Oxfordian voice was well adapted to speak for a fading English aristocracy, the perfect foil for Hitler's guttural, machine-gun staccato.

But it was Franklin Roosevelt who dominated the airwaves that year as he had ever since his first inaugural. With one speech he had reversed the mood of a nation from inertia and despair to confident action. In his fireside chats over the radio he seemed to be talking to each of us personally and we responded. Hearing his voice, we sensed a gallant, generous-spirited human being, not a party hack or a synthetic product packaged by Madison Avenue. For that brief decade we tasted democracy and the taste was good. The country recovered its health, materially and spiritually. Then came the war and other policies, often masking as his, and the taste turned bitter.

The scope and power of radio were increased manifold by the advent of television. The images and voices that enter our home over invisible electronic waves have an element of magic. The shadow of a speaker on a screen can be more persuasive than if he were present in person and his voice can carry to the corners of the earth. Never has there been such an opportunity for the dissemination of knowledge. The world passes before this small window in our living room; the best minds of our time can educate us in their special fields of learning.

But the obverse is also true We can have thrust upon us a false picture of reality as distorting as the trick mirrors in a Coney Island funhouse. In the realm of politics we are especially vulnerable. The politician can bend the airwaves to create an image of himself and of the world that suits his purposes. Nor can we question him or answer back. His is the privileged voice and we its captured audience.

In early, less complicated, times politics was a game in which we participated only for a few weeks each year until a winner emerged on the first Tuesday in November. But now the stakes have become too high, it is no longer a game and its effects are with us in some form from birth to death. Politics is in the air we breathe and in the price of bread; politics can determine how we live and how we die, even whether the earth will remain habitable for our race to evolve or whether the twentieth century will be our last.

During World War I Clemenceau made the often quoted remark that war was too serious a business to be left to the generals. Similarly today, politics has become far too serious a matter to be left to the politician. Through the mass media he has access to the minds of millions of people; with the assistance of public relations experts he can color facts and recreate history to suit himself. When logic is clearly against a policy he is trying to sell, he can fall back on an emotional appeal to loyalty and patriotism. By clever manipulation people can

IF THE MARTIANS HAD WON

*"This is Glub, sitting in for Tom Dunn on the 'Eleven O'Clock News,'
and I wish to announce that there has been a rather sudden and
sweeping change in your government."*

be made to swallow poison — literally and figuratively — if administered in small doses, carefully timed, and with the label of an accepted authority.

When Shaw said democracy might well be the best form of government if it were ever tried, he meant that an electoral majority is no indication of an enlightened choice unless the electorate is correctly informed on the issues and educated to their own interests. From recent experience we know that we have very little to say in the selection of political candidates since the nominees for public office are pretty well determined in the higher financial and party circles. Too often we are forced to vote for a lesser evil instead of a greater good.

It has been claimed that people get the government they deserve but I believe this is unfair to the general run of human beings whose personal morality is usually on a higher plane than the political ethic. The average man shows great intelligence and aptitude in those areas where he is not inhibited by fear or prejudice. Listen to a football fan analyze the intricacies of a game or watch an amateur chess player anticipate the objectives behind his adversary's moves. In a situation where the elements are within his immediate purview he has the demonstrated capacity for cause and effect analysis. Why then is he such easy prey for the political demagogue?

Part of the answer, I believe, lies in the fact that he must rely on sources of information that may or may not be correct. Even more inhibiting to an objective appraisal is the sacrosanct character in which we have invested authority throughout history, whether king, emperor, president, general or prince of the church. His position, however attained or how irresponsibly used, guarantees an automatic, unthinking allegiance from a large part of the population.

We would not consider going to a doctor who had not taken the required medical courses nor would we want a lawyer who had never been to law school, nor an untrained teacher for our children. Even a plumber has to pass certain requirements before he can be licensed. Yet we entrust our fortunes and our lives to men who have had no specific training in the most important science of all — that of governing. By all rights, politics should be the hardest profession to enter; applicants for public service should be subjected to the most rigid disciplines and tests in the psychological and social sciences as well as the humanities. Because of the years of preparation this would involve and the nature of their responsibilities, they should be the highest paid of all professions. On the other hand, they should receive no campaign contributions or other financial benefits of any kind that could subject them to pressures from special interest lobbies.

If a doctor were to prescribe certain drugs because of some profitable connection with the pharmaceutical corporation that manufactures them, he would be considered unethical and in danger of losing his license to practice. In politics no such ethic exists. The average public official climbs the political ladder by virtue of deals and promises, implicit or otherwise, which later have to be paid off in appointments and concessions to his more powerful backers, often at the expense of the public.

Changing politics from a wheeling-and-dealing popularity contest into a science presupposes an ideal state which isn't likely to come into existence in the foreseeable future. Meanwhile, how can we protect ourselves from politically biased information coming to us through the mass media? It isn't as simple as dialing another station as in the case of the Martian scare. In my opinion, the only safeguard we have is the cultivation of a skeptical attitude toward all authority, to regard no person or office sacrosanct, to accept nothing that doesn't accord with our experience and our knowledge acquired from other sources.

Most of my generation were brought up to give unquestioned obedience to authority, whether parental, religious or political. The result has been a compliant and conformist society that has tolerated a war every decade, all sorts of racial and economic inequities and a progressive spoliation of our planet. The management, shall we say, has been less than perfect.

But for the first time there are signs of a change and we have good reason to hope that the world won't be lost by default. Today all authority is being questioned and challenged, especially by the young. The American people have become more concerned with public affairs on every level. They are taking less on faith; the individual intelligence is beginning to assert itself in self-protection — and therein lies the promise of a society with the attributes for survival.

If the nonexistent Martians in the broadcast had anything important to teach us, I believe it is the virtue of doubting and testing everything that comes to us over the airwaves and on the printed pages — including those written by the author of this book.

8